Bangles

Bangles

May 11, 2017

To Yuri,
Thanks for all of your help and smiles; we will miss you.

Love,
Marsha Marie
"Jasmine"

A Memoir by

Marsha Marie

Published by Y. K. 'Marsha Marie', Arizona

Email: marsha@marshamarie.com

Printed in U.S.A.

Visit the author's website at www.marshamarie.com.

First Edition

This is a work of nonfiction. The events are portrayed to the best of Y. K.'s, aka Marsha Marie, memory. While all of the stories in this book are true, most names have been changed to protect the privacy of the people involved.

Edited by Emily Wasek, Kimberly Linkletter and Carlie Noël Sorosiak. Formatting and book cover by Word-2-kindle.com.

To my loving and amazing mother, Sandi. I can still feel you with me.
And to my children, Mona, Shedi and Nudul.
I love you all beyond words.

Hardships often prepare ordinary people for an extraordinary destiny.
....C.S. Lewis

Contents

Acknowledgments...9

Foreword 10

Introduction..13

Surrender..15

Thinking 29

The Decision...34

Ancient Ruins 39

What Kind of Tea?...48

Aunti...53

Going Solo 56

The Kitchen..62

Drive-Up Munja Night...72

Knock Knock 77

Cow Patties...81

Am I Dying? 83

Animal Kingdom..87

The Tonga 91

Laundry...95

Arrest Number One 97

Two Golden Bangles 101

Tough Love 106

Voodoo Chicken..111

All I Want 117

Godi Mommi 120

Welfare Check 124

The Lie 128

300 Falling Stars 133

Heart Attack 137

Say What? 141

Beverly Hillbillies 145

The Truce 148

Mr. Rizvi 156

Heaven or Hell? 158

Run! 162

I Am An American! 165

My Greatest Loss 169

Unlikely Visitor 171

Celebrities 174

Most Embarrassing Moment Award 177

Time to Return 180

Welcome Home Marsha 187

Phoenix 189

Gallery 191

Acknowledgments

I would like to thank all of those who have encouraged me to pen my story, especially my daughter, Mona, my toughest audience and critic. She envisioned so much, and brought out the author in me that I could not see. Also, thanks to my son, Shedi, for growing up and being there for me to lean on. He is now *my* tower of strength.

A special thanks, *shukria*, to Amijon and Roni, for teaching me how to survive in Kalu. I will always love them for that.

A huge thanks to my attorney, Duane Cates, for his support and counsel through the years.

A very special thanks to my amazing editor, Emily Wasek; her editing helped take my writing to a whole new level.

I'd also like to thank all of my beta readers who took the time to read and review my early drafts; their patience and observations were invaluable.

Thanks to all of my glorious friends, adopted families, and students— around the planet—that I fell in love with along my incredible journey.

And lastly, thank *you*, the reader, for taking the time to hear my side of the story and laugh with me about these crazy things in my life—impossible as they may seem. Feel free to shake your head in amazement at the things you're about to discover about me. (I *still* do.)

Foreword

There are moments in life when you know you've stumbled upon a real gem like some seven years ago when I met this fabulous American woman— Marsha "Yasmine" Marie. And she's not just a gem, she's a diamond that's one-of-a- kind!

In today's world of infidelity, dishonesty, and hatred, it's not just luck to find a real friend. It's like winning the jackpot. I've never really trusted people enough to make real friends. One could even say I've always had some trust issues, mostly because people show more hatred and jealousy than support and care. That was one of the reasons why I decided to leave my home country, Bulgaria, and become somewhat self-dependent by moving to the Middle East. Going from an Eastern European country still struggling to abolish socialism to the United Arab Emirates was a real eye-opener, and quite a revelation of how difficult life could be.

I can vividly recall the first time that I met Marsha. It was one of those extremely hot (especially for me!) days in April when you feel that it should be spring, but it instead feels like the hottest summer already. I was employed to work at a college and couldn't wait to start my teaching career. I took a taxi and went straight to the place where I was about to start work in and headed for the manager's office. And right there, in the reception area was Marsha, dressed in her regular ankle-length coat and covered with a beautiful pink head scarf.

Her face was shining with one of her sweetest smiles, and her eyes were like the deepest blue sea. I knew instantly she couldn't be Arabic or any other locally- grown descent. She was too strikingly different. At the time, my Bulgarian colleague, Anna, and I weren't entirely sure what was expected of us not only as English teachers, but as women and members of the UAE society. It turned out we were to follow a certain code of conduct, which Marsha revealed to us. She guided us through the culture and customs of the UAE, and helped us learn how important it was to follow the local rules and regulations.

Later on, I reflected on the importance of actually knowing more about the ethnicity and culture of the countries you've decided to visit, but at the time when I travelled to the UAE, I didn't know much about it. Marsha guided me through the teaching process: the way students learned there, the expectations, the management, and all the other intricacies of working in that particular society. I knew she was special, that something had made her become that bright star she is today. With time, she opened up and told us about her life, the hardship, and the misfortunes she'd experienced. Ever since, I've been anticipating this particular moment when she would muster the courage, and write her memories, sharing her story.

There are many victims of domestic violence who can learn a lot from her experiences and find her book especially useful. Reading the book now, I've relived all the moments back then when she was telling me about the pain she'd been through when leaving the USA, the pain her second husband had caused her by taking her third baby away, and I was an unlucky witness to all of the pain her third husband was causing her quite on purpose, again and again. Her book, with all the details of her adventures in Pakistan and challenges in the UAE, sets the ball rolling for a discussion about love, friendship, parenthood, and nationality. It is a must-read for everyone, not only those suffering from domestic violence, but also those struggling to survive and succeed in life after their hardships and setbacks. The ability to pick yourself up with your head up and self-confidence intact is vital and is one thing that Marsha does with incredible ease.

Her stories are painfully real, candid, and extremely sad, filled with the tormented feelings that only an escapee could have, feeling sorry for her lost past and homeland; filled with the guilt of a parent subjecting her children to distress and anxiety; and filled with the anguish a daughter experiences when witnessing her loving parent's deteriorating health. But more importantly, they also reveal an immense love for her children, her mother, and mother-in-law; her incorrigible and infective humor; and her incredible strength to endure and overcome any hurdles upon her way and arise from the ashes like a phoenix. Even though when reading through this book, one can often sense the standstill and impasse that she's been through dozens of times, one can also see that Marsha effortlessly takes control of her life and feels empowered by her experiences, the lessons she's learnt, and the difficulties she's encountered. She's not only a source of support for herself and her children, but a role model of vitality and success for her followers, too. This book isn't about the dark side of domestic violence, but the power and determination one should have to keep going and never give up.

Stanislava Eneva
Short Story Writer and English Instructor
Author of *Love at First Sight*
Bulgaria
June 16, 2016

Introduction

Have you ever used dirt-riddled sand to wash dishes? Have you ever had to tear your pajama bottoms in half to use as sanitary napkins? Or made crutches for your son—who had just broken his ankle—with shovel handles and washcloths? Or fled to the other side of the *planet* to get away from an ex—not once, but twice? I have.

Some sagas are too compelling to remain untold. This is absolutely one of them. Over the years, I've had several writers attempt to pen my story for me; but something was just not right. Their result wasn't what I wanted down on paper. Was I a victim of domestic violence? Absolutely. But was it what defined me? Absolutely NOT! I overcame. And despite everything, I lived a pretty amazing life outside of the United States. Yes, there were many hard days, but there were so many good days too; and I want that joy—those small victories in my life—to shine through my words as I share my story with the world.

The reason I chose to write this book is simple: I wanted my children to hear from *me* as to why I chose the primitive life I did. I wanted it to come straight from my heart.

I'm not particularly proud of *all* of the decisions that I've made in my life; but I do accept responsibility for every single one of them—good and bad. Moreover, I'm determined to make up for any lost time with all of my strength. I want to rebuild the bridges that I destroyed by my fear of speaking up when I should have. It's true that I may not be able to mend every single linkage; but those that I can, I will. It is never too late to try.

I hope that, as you read this memoir, you can feel not only the fear and the freedom that I felt along the way, but also the love and forgiveness. This is my own true and amazing account—as best as I can remember.

Bangles

(Mug Shot, March 1, 2014)

Surrender

Twenty years of running ends today—March 1, 2014. I'm sitting here on an international flight, wedged between my daughter and a young, handsome Marine going home on his leave. I'm heading towards Phoenix Sky Harbor Airport to turn myself in.

The plane ride is long and tense. I've been chatting on and off since we left Dubai, trying to keep my mind busy. I can't believe I'm finally ending this. I've taken my headscarf off for the first time in years. I feel an unusual sense of freedom, but shyness at the same time.

Mona, now twenty-five, has been my greatest support and comfort. She calls Dubai her home and rejects the idea of returning to the States, most likely because she fears what lies ahead. Nevertheless, she stays positive.

"They're not going to take you," she says, reassuring herself more than me. "You have to think positive, Mom."

"Okay, dear. I will," I say with a slight tremor in my voice.

Walking down the long carpeted hallway of the terminal, I feel as if everyone around me knows who I am—knows of what I've done. But in reality, all of the other passengers are in their own world, clambering to see who can get to the immigration counter first. The lines are lengthy, but it's just as well for me.

Wait! Is that my heart pounding? Can everyone hear it? I feel as if I am in Edgar Allan Poe's "Tell-Tale Heart." My booming chest will surely give me away, each heartbeat echoing my hidden guilt to the world.

I step up to the counter. This is it. The man asks for our passports, and I hand them over. I try to breathe, but I feel as if an elephant is sitting on my chest; it's just too heavy to bear. *"Breathe, Yasmine! Damn it!"* I internally scream to myself. *"They'll know something's up!"*

The immigration officer is wearing a typical immigration officer's uniform, safely tucked away in his little boxed-off glass area. *Tick, tick, tick,* he types on the keyboard with each stroke taking me closer to exposure. Will he discover in the system that I'm wanted by FBI? Will he know that I've been eluding the authorities for the last twenty-two years?

And then, I see it in his eyes. He does. I guess it's true; a criminal can always tell when they've been made.

He tries to make small talk with me about Dubai. But each stroke on the keyboard seems more urgent, more excited as he informs his colleagues on the other end of the intranet about me. I know on the inside that he's jumping up and down like a screaming little kid, *"I've finally caught somebody! Come and get her!"*

Suddenly, I see a large officer standing to my right. Whether he's immigration or police, I can't distinguish at this point.

"Can you go with this gentleman, ma'am?" the immigration officer says.

Slowly and steadily, we follow as I grasp Mona's hand. He leads us to a large deserted area in the terminal. About four other officers are huddled together, as if in a football game, mapping out the next play.

As I watch them, nausea sets in. After a minute or so, one of the four separates from the circle and comes towards us.

"Ma'am. Are you aware that there are two arrest warrants out for you?" the officer inquires.

"Yes, I do," I say. "Can I can get my attorney's letter out of my bag? I can show you that I'm surrendering myself—to clear all of this up."

I continue to speak as I reach in my purse for the letter, "My son should be right outside waiting for me. Can I call him?"

"No! No calls." one officer from the desk area quickly snaps back. The officer standing near me takes the letter and returns to his group.

Mona starts to tear up; the pressure is now too much. This has just gotten real for both of us. I grab her hand again and hold tight—a feeble move to calm a young woman with autism who hasn't been separated from her mother in the last twenty-two years.

"Everything will be okay, sweetie. Don't worry, I have this all planned out. I have to turn myself in. They'll let me out in a couple of hours. This is all part of the process."

"Marsha, we've just spoken to your son outside. He's waiting for his sister," the officer informs me. "Please stand up. You're under arrest; we have to take you into custody."

The finality of it all has hammered down upon us. I embrace my daughter and try to calm her tears.

"Why are they taking you? You've done nothing wrong!" she bursts, unable to bear silence any longer.

I try to calm her. "Sweetie," I say. "Your brother is just outside the airport. This officer will take you to him. Okay? I'll be fine. This is what I came back to do. I have to do this. For all of us."

The officer leads my precious Mona away from me—out of the terminal and towards her awaiting brother. She is sobbing. My heart is breaking. My legs go numb, and I have to sit down. A female officer comes towards me and asks me to stand back up, then handcuffs both of my hands behind my back. The clasps of the cuffs echo through the empty terminal. I'm escorted to the awaiting police vehicle outside.

The cuffs are cold and hard, making it difficult for me to sit in the back cab of this small pick-up truck. The escorting officer bizarrely asks me about Dubai. "Yeah," he says, "I've always thought about going there."

"Really?" I reply, almost reminiscent, with a touch of regret for having just left. "It really is an amazing place."

***

I'm in my holding cell. Could this be any smaller? The walls are made of cement block, with a cement shelf built into the back of it. The shelf is about two and a half feet off the ground. The entire room is painted a shade shy of daisy-yellow, and the door is oversized and metal. A female officer un-cuffs me and asks if I would like a drink of water.

"Yes. Please," I barely utter. "This room is awfully small. Can you leave the door open for me? I'm extremely claustrophobic."

The woman very politely—and surprisingly—agrees. (You never know when you'll get what you ask for it.)

I sit on the cold, hard shelf, like an obedient child who has just been given a time out, and watch them as they cluster around the desk reading and discussing my profile on two different computer screens. I eventually get tired of trying to eavesdrop, and look around to size up the room.

"Six feet by four. Yuck! Please God, don't let them shut the door," I pray under my breath with all sincerity.

"Is it true?" I hear suddenly. I look up and see one of the officers is slightly leaning against the metal doorframe, with his arms crossed. "Are you really surrendering yourself after running for twenty-two years?"

"Yes," I say, without even a touch of pride.

"That took a lot of courage," he replies. "Well, I think you're doing the right thing by turning yourself in. Don't worry. This'll all be just a memory in the morning."

After a while, the female officer returns. "We're going to transfer you to the main city jail now. I'll have to put the handcuffs on you again."

I stand up and go along without any kind of hesitation. One of the male officers escorts me out to the transporting wagon and opens the little cab area between the driver's seat and the back cage. He guides me in. It's cold and dark—almost black. The seats are hard plastic and my hands hurt pressing against them. I try to scoot over, but the long, tight skirt I'm wearing is only complicating matters. I half lean over and my head rests on the side of the cab just behind the driver's side; my feet are still behind the passenger's side. I give up on trying to move any further. The only light I can see is from the streetlights looking out the front windshield through the metal screen that separates me from the front. Suddenly, I feel true isolation for the first time in my life. Never before have I felt such intense loneliness. I begin to weep softly.

A few seconds later, I hear a voice coming from behind me. "Mom. Whadja do?"

I'm a bit taken back as I hear this young, male voice coming from sheer darkness. Not knowing if I'm annoyed that someone is getting up in my business, or relieved to hear a human voice in my darkest moment, I barely give the effort to turn my head to see who is speaking to me.

Oh, what do I even say to THAT? I don't reply but continue to sob.

He says, "Oh, Mom, don't worry. Everything's gonna be okay. You'll see the judge in the morning and you'll get to go home. Morning will be here before you know it."

Then the voice goes silent again. A driver climbs in the front and we're off. I peer out my screened opening to see if I can recognize Phoenix. I recognize nothing.

***

We arrive at the main city jail. I continue through a rigorous and callous check-in process, from one small holding cell to the next—all serving different functions: mouth swabbing, groping, finger-printing and, of course, the infamous mug shot. Like controlling cattle, the door opens to one of my holding cells. The officer calls my name and tells me to stand behind the podium for my picture to be taken—leaving me open for yet another opportunity of inquiry.

"So-o," the officer says, all drawn out. "I hear that you've been hiding out for over twenty years. Is that true?"

"I'm not proud of what I have done," I murmur.

With amazement in his voice and almost a chuckle, he says, "Well, you're either *really* good, or we're *really* bad?" It almost sounds like he wants me to answer the question, but then he quickly adds, pointing at the card taped below the camera, "Go ahead and look at this card right here." *Snap!* "Turn." *Snap!*

After the mug shot, the officer instructs me to go to the nurse's station. This main function area is now co-ed.

A female nurse sits behind a huge desk. She's wearing a typical white nurse's uniform. She looks over at me and says, "I'm going to ask you some questions and you just answer. Okay?"

I shake my head, agreeing, another tear streaming down my face.

"Do you smoke?"

"No."

"Do you use marijuana?"

"No."

"Do you use heroine?"

"No."

"Have you ever shared a needle with anyone?"

"No. Really, are all of these questions necessary?"

"I'm sorry, but I have to ask them." She continues, "Have you ever been a prostitute?"

"No!"

"Have you... Have you... Have you...?" The questions keep coming.

"No...no...no...." I answer with mirroring rhythm.

Finally, the nurse says, "You know what? Looking down this list, I don't think we need to continue. I can already tell what the answers are..."

Her words are suddenly cut off as a mammoth of a man inside the holding cell directly behind me starts slamming his fists on the metal doors and screaming profanities at the top of his lungs. I jump in surprise as fear strikes through me as lightening. I begin crying even harder—but now out of terror. The man keeps pounding and pounding on the door. Three officers bellow at him to calm down. He doesn't stop. The door flies open. They tackle the man and start tazing him.

My entire body is literally shaking by this point. "I don't belong here!" I sputter at the nurse, knowing very well that she can't help me.

She leans in closer to me over the desk and says, "Do you want to know how to survive in here?"

I shake my head as if to say yes.

"Just focus inward. Try to block out everything that's happening around you out. Okay? You'll make through the night."

(Again, a voice of reason comes to me when I most need it).

She continues, "It's nice seeing someone that really doesn't belong in here—if you know what I mean."

I nod, wiping another tear away. "Thank you."

I get up and walk to the next processing station. I take a seat at the beginning of the long bench. As we're called, we move down to the right. In due time, I make it to the end of the bench. My tears have dried for now. A young boy seats himself next to me. I continue looking forward.

Suddenly, I hear him say, "Are you okay, Mom?"

With instant recognition, I look up to towards the boy. It's the same voice I heard in the dark hole from before. With a half-smile, I reply, "Yeah. Yeah, I'm okay."

"Has anyone told you what will happen tonight?"

"No. No one."

"Once you're done here, you'll go out into the hall in the next room. They'll search you again and then take you to another cell for the rest of the night. Then, in the morning you'll see the judge, and then you'll get out. Don't worry. It'll go by fast."

"Thanks. What's your name?"

"Kevin."

"Thanks, Kevin."

Again they call my name and take me to the next hall just as Kevin had said.

"Stand here, young lady. Remove your coat and shoes," the beckoning officer politely instructs me.

A female officer heads over with surgical gloves on.

Oh my god. What is she gonna do?

She stands directly in front of me and says, "Bend over at the waist and hang your arms straight down."

I oblige without saying a word.

"I'm sorry for doing this," she apologizes in advance.

She runs her fingers along the bottom inside of each cup in my bra. She then grabs the middle area where the cups are joined, and shakes it to and fro.

Then, she says, "Now put your hands against the wall."

Another patting down.

Again? How many times are we gonna do this tonight?

"Alright, put your stuff back on and stand against that wall."

The officer then leads me down the hall into my next holding tank. It's about two a.m., and there are about twenty-five women sleeping sprawled out on the benches and the floor. The room has two phones on the wall to my right, and a u-shaped cement bench to the left. There's a toilet against the back wall and a green thirty-gallon garbage can by the toilet. *How odd.* I find a narrow spot along the middle of the u-shaped bench and settle in—there's nothing to do but wait for my attorney to arrive.

As women often do, I carefully chose my wardrobe for my return to Phoenix. Unfortunately, I didn't consider that I might have to sleep on the floor of the city jail. I'm wearing my favorite long Turkish black skirt with a black turtleneck shirt, my bluish-purple power-blazer, black high-heels, and—to top it off just right—a long, multi-colored stone necklace. Maybe I over-thought it just a bit—and by the looks of it, I'm the only one who did. Some of the women have dirty jeans on, some shorts and tank tops. One lady even has her house slippers on. But the thing freaking me out the most is this young girl who's scratching and shaking. Forget her dirty clothes; she has scabs all over her body.

The cement holding cell is chilly, with a dirty brown cement floor, and a pungent metallic smell. Suddenly, my claustrophobia kicks in. I find it harder and harder to breathe. My eyes begin dashing to and fro, looking for a passage for air. They lock onto the two-inch space under the steel door. I convince myself that the air coming from under the door is just for me. I can actually see it flowing towards me; it's invisible, but I can see it.

"Okay, calm down. You can do this. Breathe... Breathe..." I say to myself, between each long gulp of air. I start to relax. My breathing stabilizes.

One of the girls gets up and uses the toilet. *Oh my. Am I supposed to look the other way?* After she finishes, she lies down in a different spot. I notice a depleted roll of toilet paper next to me. The other girls are using the rolls of paper as pillows. *I'd better take that and keep it with me for later.* I slyly snatch the roll and press it flat, stuffing the roll into the left front facing of my blazer. *Okay, now I'm ready just in case.*

(That stash of toilet paper came in very handy later that night, as the call of nature came to light in the most inappropriate way for public display. I tried to scrape up *some self-respect* by using the garbage can as a barrier. Not one of the finest moments of my life.)

Around five a.m., we're suddenly jarred alert by an officer at the door. He yells out that it's time to eat. Like a scene out of a horror movie, the women begin rising from the floor and take a spot on the bench. *I wonder what they serve in jail.* The officer leads a young man in an orange prisoner jumpsuit holding an open box with clear baggies spiking out the top; he couldn't be more than twenty-four years old. Without uttering a word, he walks around to each woman in the cell and offers them the three items from the menu tonight: one small bottle of fruit juice, one hamburger bun, and one baggie with a few tablespoons of creamy peanut butter.

The two "waiters" leave the cell and the women begin devouring. I decide that it's best to ration. *Who knows when my next meal will be?* So, I take a few bites of the bread, and suck on some of the peanut butter for flavor. I savor it slowly, and then down it with a small swish of juice. Once the women have finished, they return to their spots on the floor and benches, and drift back off to sleep again. I sit silently in the same spot, thinking. Keeping my food supply near—and just thinking.

***

Time crawls its way to morning and the sound of the keys rouse me. *Finally. Maybe it's time to see the judge?* They call out a list of names. *Yes! Thank God!* I wait anxiously for my next instruction. An officer tells us to line up against the wall outside in the hallway. With my peanut butter and juice bottle in tow, I accept my place in line and follow the lead. We walk slowly with no sudden movements into a small white room. Again, they take my fingerprints.

A female officer looks at my food and says while pointing to a trash can, "You can't take that with you inside to see the judge. You need to dump it here."

There goes my food supply.

The officer leads us into the courtroom next door. It's cold, and much brighter compared to the holding block—mostly white floor and walls.

Hey, where's my lawyer? I look around and keep thinking that he will come into view at any minute, but he isn't anywhere in sight. The proceedings begin.

A recorded male voice comes over the speaker: "You have a right to…" The words fade into the background. I whip my head to and fro. *Where is my attorney?* He's nowhere in sight.

A female judge, sitting on a circular brown platform, calls my name with authority.

"Marsha Marcum." I walk to the marked spot as one does on a performance stage. "State your name and date of birth, please," the judge commands.

My voice cracks as I answer her.

The judge continues, and without any explanation announces, "Because of your record, you will remain in jail until your hearing."

What? My legs go numb. Oh my God! I'm going to jail? Where's my attorney? This wasn't supposed to happen like this.

Suddenly, I remember that my attorney had scheduled a quash warrant hearing for me. I finally muster the courage to speak to the judge.

"But, Your Honor. I came to America for a quash hearing," I say with great desperation. "I thought my attorney would be here for me right now, but he isn't, and I don't have his number with me. My purse went home with my children."

"Okay. Let me look into it. Go back and sit down. The bench will call you up when I am ready."

My mind is racing a thousand words a minute. I begin mumbling to myself, "I shouldn't have come back home. This was not supposed to happen like this. Where is my attorney? Oh God, what have I done?"

After what seems like hours, but in reality is only about thirty minutes, the judge calls me back to the bench again. "We looked into it, and yes, you do have a hearing set in a few days. I'll go ahead and release you."

Oh, thank God! "Thank you, ma'am," I say.

***

I 'm transferred to one processing room after another. Each room is getting smaller than the one before. I wait anxiously to be released. I'm still trying to fathom what in the world happened to my attorney. *Why didn't he show up?* I ask myself over and over again. We'd planned this out for well over a year.

The final processing room has a phone in it. I try to call my son to let him know that I'm being released, but I can't remember the bloody number. I think as hard as I can, but it's just not coming to me. Luckily, one of the other girls being released is calling her mother on the phone next to me. I ask her if her mother could go onto Facebook and let my son know what is happening—it's worth a shot, anyway. After twenty minutes, her mother has found him.

"He's on his way," she says.

Awesome!

***

At last, I'm released from jail. I step outside with great anticipation, but nothing greets me except a light shower of rain. Still, I'm not sad. I'm back home. I've made it to America. These cool, refreshing drops are a welcome change from my former desert refuge abroad. At last, appearing from around the corner, I see my son and daughter on American soil. We embrace. This is the first day of a lengthy legal battle, but my two children are here beside me, to love me, to support me and my past decisions.

"Son," I anxiously ask, "where's my attorney? Did you call him and tell him I was arrested at the airport?"

"Oh yeah..." he says, "I forgot."

COURT	COURT W #	COURT DATE	CNT	CHARGE		CL	BOND
SUP CRT	CR0304551		1	PROBATION VIOLATION		F6	
SENTENCE						MISC	NO BOND BW,FTC
COURT	COURT W #	COURT DATE	CNT	CHARGE		CL	BOND
SUP CRT	CR9707679		2	CUSTODIAL INTERFERENCE		F6	104000.00
SENTENCE						MISC	GJ
COURT	COURT W #	COURT DATE	CNT	CHARGE		CL	BOND
SENTENCE						MISC	
PROPERTY ID TYPE/NO(US PASSPORT); MISC PAPERS (ONE SHEET OF PAPER)						CASH	
						CLASSIFICATION	
AKAS YASMINE				ARREST AGENCY A200/2300	OR # DR - YES		
SCARS / MARKS / TATOOS			LOCKER	AR OFF # 5083	IN OFF # 8094	BK OFF # PHX20	ARREST NUMBER 1402281030	ARREST DATE & TIME 02/28/14 204?
LAST NAME MARCUM	FIRST MARSHA	MI V	SUF	BOOKING DATE & TIME 03/01/14 0223	LOCATION INTROTA		BOOK # T058076

(My arrest paperwork. Notice, the only property that I had was my passport and the letter from my attorney.)

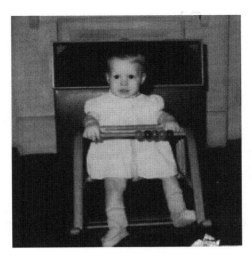

(1966)

Thinking

I was born in Ohio in the summer of 1965. My mother's name was Sandi ("with an 'i'" she always insisted) and she was absolutely amazing. She played the guitar and was an avid dancer. She was always there for me when I needed her. Now and again, I can still hear her calling me. "Sissie!" (She called me Sissie most of the time, not Marsha.)

We are all products of our past; be it good or bad. My mother's youthful memories were stolen away by sickening acts of abuse by her drunken father. Over time, she was able overcame the tragedy, but continued to bear the deep, painful scars of her childhood. I know that she was determined, with all of her heart, not to let that violent abuse bleed over into another generation. I know she tried her best. But my father only added insult to injury. His violent outbursts were managed by his abuse of steroids. They divorced when I was five, so the few memories I do have of him were mostly loud and bloody.

I was a sickly baby and wasn't able to drink milk like I was supposed to. The doctor instead prescribed carrot juice. I drank so much of it, that my skin developed an orange tint.

By the time I was two, I had been hospitalized with pneumonia several times. The doctors encouraged my parents to move me to a warmer, drier climate—thus; Phoenix, Arizona became my new home.

Let's fast-forward a bit. When I was fifteen years old, I first met David at our apostolic church, but we didn't start dating until I was eighteen. He was tall and lanky like his father—who was an elder in the church and led song worship; his father even had his own prison ministry at one point. Unfortunately, these compassionate traits didn't rub off onto his son. David was a rock-n-roll rebel, and I was very immature and foolish. It was a well-known fact that David displayed aggressive behavior towards those around him. But I wouldn't listen to my closest friends, or clergy—I was in love. So, against all warnings, we eloped in 1985.

Well, I could drabble on and on about my ex, but this book is not about him or his many demons. It's about me—accepting responsibility for the many choices I've made in my life. So, to protect everyone involved, I've changed everyone's name in this memoir except my own (and a few of those who gave special permission).

(My son's baby dedication with Rev. Ray Brown in Truth Tabernacle,
Avondale, Arizona. May 1988)

I remember my internal struggles and sadness like it was yesterday…

I sit alone on the pew with two babies, one two-year-old beautiful
daughter, and a six-month-old bouncing boy. The church has about a
hundred visitors today and we're sitting in our usual spot near the back.
The music is playing loudly. Suddenly, the dread of going home envelopes
me again. I look around at other couples who have been married for years.
They're happy and have made perfect little families. This is the same church
where years ago David and I first dedicated our children to God when I
still loved him. But now the violence and negativity has become too heavy
to bear. Years ago, I thought that if I gave him some time, then he'd calm
down, that things would get better. But they haven't. And now I have two
small children. God forbid I bring any more babies into this misery.

As the minister begins preaching, my thoughts again wander. *Why do I
tolerate his behavior? The anger, the road-rage, his endless control, the hitting, kicking,*

cruelty….please God, I can't live like this. Maybe, if I could just be better, then it would all stop?

The preaching continues louder, the volume helping me think even deeper. This is a safe haven for me. No one will question what I am thinking.

I don't want this marriage anymore. But I can't divorce him either, right? It's my duty to stay with him, right? Oh God, there's no way out! The only way to stop this pain is to end my life. I hang my head in surrender. *But I can't do that, either. The kids need me. I can't leave my babies behind.*

The preaching ends and I go home like I always do. I play the role of obedient homemaker—cooking, cleaning, and… well, you get the idea.

***

Months go by. Nothing has changed. I still keep my secrets of David's anger and obsessive control from the outside world, learning how to survive and hide my sadness. David had been saying that I was overweight since the time we got married, so I tried my best to lose some; but now, I find myself actually addicted to dieting and aerobic exercise. I work out three times a day—mostly in the kitchen and the living room. David is finally pleased with my new look and his comments have ended. However, my seventy-five pound weight loss has started upsetting my mother. She says that at 117 pounds, I don't look healthy anymore. But at this point in my life, eating—or in this case *not* eating—seems to be the only thing in life that I can control.

All I know is that I want out of the house and by any means. I think a job is the perfect answer. After days of pleading, I am able to convince David to let me get a part-time job. I return to the same hardware store where I used to work before we were married. He only allows me to work weekends, but I am happy with that small victory. It is something to get me out of the house—even if it is only for a couple of hours a week. It's a relief to get away.

It is here that I run into an old flame of mine, Zain. We met five years earlier—ironically, at the very same store. He'd seemed exotic to me at the time; he was young, handsome and from Pakistan, with a heavy accent. We'd had a strange, instant attraction, but things between us just didn't work out and we went our separate paths.

Meeting up again in the same store is an exhilarating experience for both of us. He tells me that he has finally been following his dream of directing movies in Hollywood and that he is living between Phoenix and L.A. He tells me all about his new life in California, and about all of the TV shows in which he has been doing bit parts. We talk in the aisle of the store for about an hour. I am delighted for him. I don't let on anything about my problems at home. I'm sure I'll never see him again anyway—so why say anything of my depressing abusive marriage? Secret still intact.

The Decision

As it turned out, Zain and I kept in touch. Our talks got longer and longer each time—both in *and* out of the store. We reminisced about our previous relationship and laughed about how five years had gone by so fast. Finally, I felt comfortable enough to speak up. I confided in him about what was happening at home. Although I knew it was wrong, I'd found in Zain the comfort my heart craved. During our moments together, he suggested that life could be different for me. "No man should hit a woman," he said.

Was he right? Could I possibly get away from the anger and the disgust that I felt at home? Could I have my own life again? I was confused and scared.

After long and hard consideration, I surrendered to the yearnings of my heart and asked David for a divorce. David tried his best to convince me not to go through with it, but my love for him was already dead. There was nothing on which to build another relationship. We ultimately decided to share custody fifty-fifty, but his controlling nature hadn't changed. His anger and control still bled into my new life.

Zain and I became closer every day. He took me to meet his family in Arizona and I fell in love with them instantly. To me, it looked as if they were twenty people living happily together in harmony.

"How is that possible?" I'd ask my mother. (You see, our family was much different. Our family's holidays often involved police intervention; it was just who we were.)

But with Zain's family, they ate together, studied together, and laughed together. It was a big happy family, such a contrast to my own life.

It was 1990, and Zain was in the middle of directing and producing a movie in Los Angeles. I got to meet a lot of people during the casting. I really didn't like the business of making movies, but it was fun actually being *in* the movie. Each weekend, I'd fly out to Hollywood to be on the set and spend time with him at the beach. It was romantic and intoxicating. Being the *director's girlfriend* afforded many perks. For instance, I got to do anything I wanted on the set, like eat everything in sight, and sit and chat with the actors for hours while they were setting up for scenes. It was fun.

In the actual movie, I got to dance at a pool party, pretend I was talking to people, and I even got to wear my own Pakistani clothing: a blue silky *salwar kameez* with a long flowing scarf to match—I'm sure I looked like the Bollywood Diva, Aishwarya Rai that day. In one particular scene, I was walking around the pool of this incredible Beverly Hills home, pretending to talk to the man walking with me. (It very well could have been Johnny Depp, or even David Spade for that matter. Just saying.) But anyway, all I could think at that time was, *Please, God. Don't let me fall in the pool in front of all these cameras.* It was a B-rated movie for sure, but still fun to be part of.

Zain eventually asked me to marry him, and I accepted. We had a traditional Pakistani wedding in Phoenix, and I wore the customary red Pakistani-style dressing, with henna tattooing and all. The wedding lasted for seven days; each day had a different role in the ceremony. I didn't understand all of the commotion, or the lengthy schedules, but it was entertaining—the longest seven days of my life. I was exhausted.

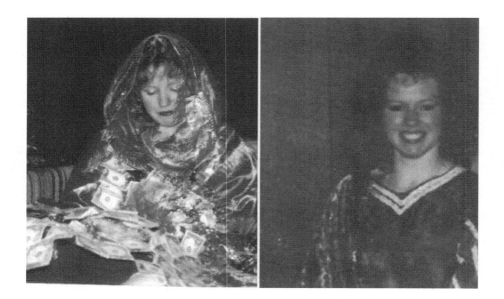

(Actual wedding and reception pictures.)

Although the lights and glam of Hollywood were exhilarating, and my wedding was something right out of Bollywood, David's mental torment continued. Always having to know where I was, what I was doing, what the kids were doing while they were with me, and so on. He even had me wear a beeper so he could page me anytime, day or night.

One day, after I hung up the phone from another invasive conversation with David, I shouted, "God, when is he ever gonna leave me alone? How can I get away from this person?"

Zain suddenly offered, "We could go live with my family? He can't bother you there."

"Oh. How's that gonna help? Same city. Hello-o?" I said a bit sarcastically.

"No, not here. In Pakistan."

"Wait. Are you serious?" I was shocked.

"Yeah."

"But how can I do that?" My mind was trying to compute what he was saying. Leaving the States with the children would mean going against the custodial agreement with David, and the last thing I want is legal trouble.

He proceeded to tell me his ideas. Then, like a fool, without any outside consultation, I went along with his plan.

My next few months were a secretive blur—making necessary preparations for our departure. I began packing for this new mysterious land (necessities—like clothes, shampoo and my Weird Al Yankovic cassette tape collection—still a huge fan by the way!). Then it came time to tell my family. It was difficult to say goodbye. My aunt took me to see the movie *Not Without My Daughter*—a movie about an American mother trapped in Iran; and then told me to be careful not to get myself sold into sex slavery. My mother stayed with me from the moment I told her I was leaving until the very last second I boarded the plane. She had an abundance of recommendations and opinions for me, but her greatest advice was "Never lose your identity!"

I thoughtlessly replied, "Oh. Okay, Mom, I won't," not understanding that these words would later transform me and ultimately save my life.

The day that we boarded the plane, my nerves were on end, and my stomach was in my throat. My son, Shedi was just over three years old, and Mona would be turning five in a few days. During the flight, Zain filled the time by trying to prepare me for my new life—telling me all about his village and family. But as I found out later, nothing could've prepared me for what I was about to discover. What a way to start a new year—1992—a new country, a new family and a new name—Yasmine, a beautiful and refreshing name that would reflect my new life.

(Me, with my new family in Kalu Kalan, Pakistan. 1992. We're standing directly in front of the kitchen and the torn down room where Zain was born. Sponge rollers? I say, never leave home without them!)

Ancient Ruins

Another twelve hours in flight and we finally arrived in Pakistan. There seemed to be a thousand people at Islamabad Airport. The terminal was unwelcoming: brown walls and a metal ceiling. The roar of an unknown language swept through the congested area. Several luggage carousels filled the center. Zain said that we'd have to be quick getting our bags so that they wouldn't be stolen. I kept a tight grip on both of the kids and followed him very closely.

We walked outside of the rustic terminal to an ocean of people. To be honest, I thought they were all there for us. I was in shock. *How big is his family?* Strangers from all different directions were grabbing me and hugging me. A few of the family members swept the kids away from me. I screamed out, shaking my head in feverish disapproval, trying to grab them back, "Wait! No, no!" I refused to let go.

"Don't worry, that's my sister!" Zain shouted over the noise.

The crowd led us to a train of vans that had brought the clan to the airport. The family started climbing into them. One after another. It was like clowns at the circus climbing into a small car. Eventually, it was my turn to join. I ended up crowded into a backseat, sitting by one of my sisters-in-law. She was young and still displaying bridal adornments. The ride home was interrupted several times by her bouts of vomiting; it turned out she was pregnant. A welcoming sound, indeed.

The journey from the airport was noisy—*very* noisy. I remember looking out the window just as the sun was rising. I could see a sprinkle of shops along the two-lane road. They looked like makeshift shacks with metal roofs slightly sloping towards the back of the store. The fog was nippy and moist, but not too dense to see through. There were no city streetlights along the road, only fluorescent-tubes hanging in the shops. Only a few men were walking slowly in the mist. They were wrapped in twin-sized blankets and wore woolen hats. No women were out at this time of the morning—none within my view, anyway.

The long stretch of road took us along our way for about an hour and a half. Eventually we went off to a narrow paved road, which then led us to a very bumpy dirt road. I looked over to my left and spotted what I thought were ancient ruins. *Wow! I wonder who lived there.*

We jolted our way down the bumpy road, and came to a stop next to some dilapidated buildings that seemed to continue down the road.

"Awesome! We get to go look at the ruins up close? O-oo! Interesting!" I squealed with excitement. *My first adventure!*

Suddenly my husband turned around from the front seat and said, "We're here."

"Oh, great! Where are we?"

"This is my mom's house!"

"What? Did I hear you right? This is your mom's house?" I quieted in a snap—I was stunned. In hindsight, I know I should've studied a bit more before taking a leap of faith to move in with Zain's family. But, all I could really think of at the time was getting away from David's control. The thought of freedom clouded my better judgment.

A gathering of people hovered around the caravan. We left the vehicles and walked down an alley just off to the left of the vans. It was too narrow for a car, but two people could walk comfortably down it side-by-side. The walls were red brick and without any stucco. On the right-hand side of the alley was a trench—three-quarters of the way full of black slimy water. The area had a certain pungent smell. (Funny, but I would eventually grow to love and recognize this smell as the smell of home.)

The crowd led me halfway down the alley and into the second door on the right. The double wooden doors were crooked from age, with a history of dents and scrapes clearly visible. Hanging about three feet inside the door was a barrier of burlap potato sacks—roughly stitched together like patchwork—that were strung up across the yard about seven feet high, parallel with the entrance gate.

We walked around the burlap sheet and into the courtyard of my mother-in-law's home. I can still see it etched in my mind.

The property layout was square, with rooms neatly laid around the outer edges. The middle courtyard was open to the sky.

To the left of the burlap barrier was a huge cow. Her calf was tied down only a few feet away. She stood on a brick-laid floor about fifteen by fifteen feet and had a cement trough that was worn and broken in places along the edges. By the obvious patches of cement, it looked like the trough had been repaired several times.

Behind the cow's trough was a storage room where the cow stayed at night or whenever the weather was uncomfortable for her outside. It also served as storage for hay and fodder.

On top of the cow room was where the cow dung was dried in huge gumdrop-shaped blobs. Once dried, it was stored and used as firewood.

To the right of the burlap barrier was a chicken coop and a small storage room—where they kept the dried cow dung. The storage room didn't have a door on it—just a rough, stringy burlap veil to keep the rain out.

Moving along in an L-shape direction was a longer brick building with two more closet-sized rooms and an attached veranda off the end. They were the bathing room and the toilet: two different rooms for two different functions.

Under the veranda was a motor with metal pipes running up to the rustic tank on top of the building. There was also a hand pump and a small, cemented area that led excess water into a gutter—which led to the trench in the alley that I mentioned earlier.

Along the back of the property were three connected buildings. The center structure was made of mud and brick. The roof had huge wooden beams with sticks crossing over it to fill up the gaps.

On top of the sticks was a hardened mud layer that sloped forward so that the rain would run off easily. The mud-stucco on the walls was worn, but freshly painted with pastel-colored limestone. This particular room belonged to my mother-in-law, Amijon. (While on the plane, I had asked

Zain about how I should address my new mother-in-law. He told me that I should call her Amijon, which means: *respected mother* in Hindko—the local language.)

The room to the left of Amijon's belonged to my sister-in-law, Wafa. It appeared to be quite newer—made with cement and brick, and had a cement slab roof on top. There was a definite contrast between the two rooms that clearly demonstrated a change in architecture and interior design.

The room to the right of Amijon's room was half torn down. The rubble really looked like ancient ruins. It looked as if an earthquake had hit, causing the ceiling to cave in. Piles of bricks and dirt lay on the ground. The walls of this room were broken down to a third of their original size.

I climbed over the bricks to explore inside. As I looked around the exposed room, and saw several bird nests where the built-in cabinets used to store fine china. There were also small cocoon-shaped balls of black hair stuffed into the broken crevices of the walls—a custom that women partake in—as they are not allowed to burn human hair. Suddenly, something brass caught my eye. I was told that it was a pitcher from my mother-in-law's wedding dishes. Apparently, this is the room where Zain was born.

Connected to the right-front corner of this historic room was the kitchen. It was about double the size of the bathroom, with a fireplace built into the left corner. In front of it were burlap sacks—laid out like throw rugs—giving a nice warm spot to sit on winter days. Dishes were in the window on wooden plank shelving. There was no glass on the outside of the window, only wire mesh and yet another burlap covering to keep out the winter chill. Oddly, the door to the kitchen was only five feet tall, and you had to step over a six-inch threshold to get in.

There were a few trees in the yard: a couple of skinny eucalyptus trees, and one nice-sized guava tree right in front of Amijon's room. The courtyard was just dirt, nothing more.

The bathroom was an intriguing place. Its wooden-plank door opened from the right. The problem with that was, since I was coming from the left, it seemed like the door was on backwards. Then when it opened, it made an eerie creaking sound. It was locked by sliding a metal cylinder latch into a little, chiseled hole in the brick wall. The brick bearing the hole was so worn down, that if you were to push against the locked door hard enough, it would open right up with the lock still engaged.

The walls of the six-by-five toilet were painted completely black. The ceiling had beams going across with little sticks positioned together to cover it—the same as Amijon's room and the kitchen. The floor was brown cement; at least I think it was brown, or maybe it was regular cement yellowed by water stains; I really couldn't tell because the light from the bulb hanging from the ceiling was too dim. Down below the bulb, about two feet off the ground, there was a small spout that protruded out of the wall. Directly under that, was a brand new, chalky green watering can— used for cleaning yourself up after using the bathroom. Toilet paper was nowhere to be found.

The actual bowl sat inside a cement platform built in the back half of the bathroom. It was a white porcelain funnel-shaped cavity with a bumpy footrest on each side. If I looked up while squatting down, I could see a bird's nest that was safely tucked away in a sweet little niche right above the door—a cool spot for the hot summers, I suppose.

***

My first experience with the bathroom *funnel* was shocking to say the very least. At first, I would end up peeing all over my legs and feet. "Oh my God, this is disgusting!" I would yell out from inside the bathroom for all to hear. Yet, through trial and error, I finally figured the best method. First, I would take off my pants, or *salwar*, and hang them on a nail inside the bathroom. Then, I would very carefully mount the funneled abyss. Then, once I finished my business, I'd use the water to wash myself off—legs, feet and everything else. (The water mirrored the weather—sometimes freezing cold, and sometimes burning hot.) Then, once I'd completely cleaned myself up, I'd re-dress—still wet from the washing. I ended up using this method for many years. But like I said, it was trial and error.

Within the first two weeks, I came up with a brilliant idea. I requested that we bring a toilet seat home to place over the hole where the feet went. Since the funnel was in the platform anyway, it made a great little spot for me to sit down. *Eureka!* With the seat, I could utilize it as if it were a regular commode, and not have to undress each time. It sounded good theoretically speaking.

But, I soon found out there was a flaw in my plan. Oftentimes, I'd end up spilling water all over my pants, which meant that I still ended up taking them off anyway. And, on top of that, they were soaked when I put them back on.

I eventually stopped using the makeshift seat altogether and learned to squat like the rest of them—you know as they say, *when in Rome?* Now, there was one last problem to solve in my bathroom chronicles. And that was learning how to aim my *stuff* at the funnel and not on the back of it next to the wall. Again, trial and error, but I'll spare you the details. Let's just say, it was a blessing that most of the time my *stuff* was water-based.

Outside the toilet was a yellow porcelain basin in the courtyard-- with an oval mirror mounted over it— where the whole family washed up and brushed their teeth.

This area also turned out to be a real showcase for the neighbors around us.

Every single morning, several villagers would stand on top of their houses to watch my morning routine. They wouldn't say anything. They would just stand and stare. They did this for months. In the beginning, I'd get really annoyed by the attention. Sometimes I'd storm off and feel like I was an animal in a cage, or in some kind of freak show. It took a long time for me to understand that the spectators didn't mean any harm. They were just curious—that's all. So, to help matters move along a bit more quickly, I had a new bathroom for myself built inside the house for privacy.

I think it is obvious by now that bathrooms were always a drama for me in my new land. I spent a lot of time washing myself over and over again (which was not easy in the winter!). I began compiling a long list of decent workable bathrooms across the entire country. I would actually have a written plan of action for my potty breaks. At least, I would try my best. Sometimes, I was hit with emergencies and thus landing in really awful latrines—but when you've gotta go, you've gotta go, right?

The sink and the bathroom area.

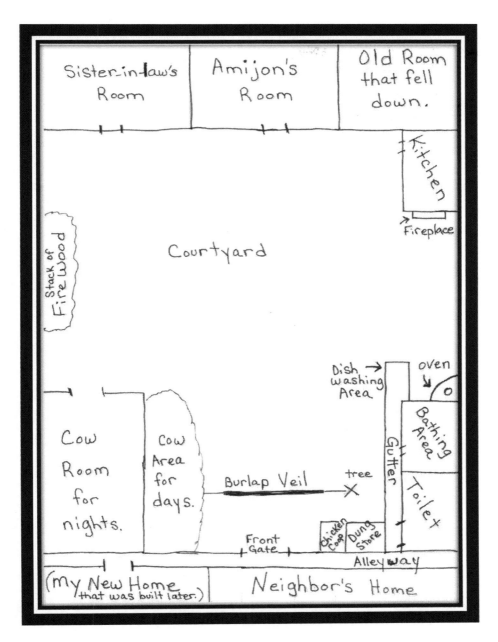

Layout of Amijon's Courtyard in 1992.

What Kind of Tea?

The name of the village we moved to is *Kalu Kalan*, but we called it *Kalu*. It's a quaint farming community. Living in Kalu was an amazing experience. Every new brick that I touched upon introduced exciting adventures and fascinating personalities. One of my favorite memories is the day I met Zain's uncle, Poopa. He was an older gentleman, probably in his seventies. He had lived in Kalu most of his life and ran a darling little general store, or *dukkan*, adjacent to his home. They lived in the center of the village and was known and loved by all. The children in the neighborhood especially loved his candy. He was a kind gentle soul, and this is how I remember our first meeting.

***

I've only been in town for about couple of weeks now. I've tried so many new foods, and seen so many new things in such a short time. It's simply invigorating. Each sunrise brings a new adventure.

"Let's go see Poopa today," says Zain.

I quickly agree, "Okay. Who's that?"

"Poopa is my uncle. He owns a little store here in town."

"Great! Let's go! First, let me get ready."

I put on my triangle scarf and the long trench coat that I've brought with me from the States.

We walk together down the dirt road of the village. I am alert like a cat, wide-eyed, soaking in my new surroundings. This is the first time that I've been down this far by foot. The road is just a bit wider than the breadth of a car, with drainage gutters on each side. They're similar to the ones in our alley, except these drains are a bit wider and deeper. There are also big mounds of black slimy sand on the road next to them.

"What's that?" I ask, pointing at one of the mounds. The smell is almost overpowering. I crinkle up my face.

"That's from the gutter, or *nally*," he explains. "When the nally gets full, the nally man comes and scoops the black slime out with a shovel and puts here for all the water to drain off. Once the water drains, then they'll load the half-dried mixture of sand and garbage onto a wheelbarrow and throw over there," he says while pointing towards a trash dumping area on the other side of the road.

"Where does all the sand come from in the first place?" I ask. "There's nothing but farms around here. I don't get it."

"The women use sand to wash the dishes. They get it from here and there; usually wherever some construction site has some just laying around."

As we walk down the road, I see small children darting in their homes with excitement; then within seconds, women are peeping out of their front gates to catch a glimpse of me. Whispers of the word "*gori*," which loosely translates to "white lady," can be heard to and fro.

Other small children are following just inches behind me, trying to hold my hand. There are too many of them; they begin pushing each other to get a turn to touch me. They are calling out my name, "*gori mommi, gori mommi!*" ("white auntie.") I'm a modern day Pied Piper.

We follow the road as it turns to the left and into Poopa's house on the corner. I stop at the door and begin to knock.

"Don't knock. Just go in," Zain says.

I'm dumbfounded. "I can't just walk in."

"We don't knock here. We just go in."

I apprehensively open the gate and step in slowly, feeling as if I am intruding or something.

Zain follows behind me and calls out, *"Booboo, Ghar hai?"* Meaning: Are you home, auntie?

His aunt comes rushing out of her main room. The home is a traditional-style home similar to Amijon's—two small rooms along the back of the property, with a courtyard—great for basking in the sun. We go directly into her room and sit down on the side of the bed, or *munja*. My legs dangle over the edge just inches above the floor.

Booboo is fluttering around making tea, and shooing the constant string of paparazzi-style children that are trying to catch a glimpse.

"We want to see *gori mommi,*" they cry out.

"Shoo, shoo! Go away!" my aunt shouts as she lunges at them, waving her arms about. The children nearly trip over each other trying to escape out the door. (This scene becomes the norm wherever I go.)

Suddenly, an elder man walks in with white *salwar kameez*, traditional Pakistani clothing, and a woolen wrap thrown over both of his shoulders. He walks straight over to Zain and greets him with an embrace. They exchange pleasant greetings in Hindko, ending with their hands over their own hearts. (Really sweet to watch.)

Poopa then walks over to me and stretches out his hand. It is wrinkled and vein-ridden. His fingers are severely curled up from his arthritis. He looks me in the eye, and I notice that one eye is lazy and very bloodshot.

With full confidence, he says to me in English, "Good morning. F... ing tea! F...ing biscuits!" (I am sure that you understand it rhymes with tucking, right? But because this is a family story, I'll keep it clean.)

I'm stunned, and speechless. My mouth drops open. I guess I take too long to respond for Poopa because within a few seconds, he flashed a huge smile and repeats, "F...ing tea! F...ing biscuits!"

Again, speechless. I look at my husband in disbelief. "Does he know what he is saying? What do I say to him?"

Zain is just as shocked. "I don't think he does. Let me ask him."

He turns back to Poopa, and they carry on a conversation for about five minutes or so. "Blah, blah, blah"—this is all I hear. Zain laughs before he finally relays the information to me.

"My uncle said that many years ago there were some British troops in this area of Pakistan. Two of the soldiers would come into his shop each morning. They would say good morning first, and then they would say, "F...ing tea! F...ing biscuits!" So, my uncle thinks that this is the way that English-speaking people greet each other. So when he saw you just now, he wanted to greet you in the *white people way*—F...ing tea! F...ing biscuits!"

We had a pretty good laugh that day. Uncle Poopa greeted me this way every single time he saw me, until his death a year later. I would simply smile each time and accept his efforts at speaking English; I thought it was so cute. He was so kind and genuine. I will never forget him.

***

Yet, it wasn't just the British that taught interesting and awkward words. My husband taught me his fair share of some Hindko phrases, too. One day, he was bored and decided to teach me *"Medi tooee krudik onihae."* He made me repeat it about twenty times, and then proudly led me around yard reciting the phrase to his family. I humored Zain because I knew he had a funny streak that ran pretty deep (and that was one of the many things I loved about him.)

One of his aunts came over to see me one day, and of course, I repeated my rehearsed script again. She started cracking up, but I still had no idea what I was saying. I figured it had to have been something hilarious by the way people laughed aloud whenever I said it to them. Finally, I had to know. So, I asked Zain, "What am I saying to them, anyway?"

"Oh," he said slyly. "*Medi tooee krudik onihae* means: My butt itches."

Honestly, I was not surprised at all.

Aunti

Pakistan had its fair share of refugees. Many of them were from Afghanistan. One particular family made Kalu their winter homeland. They weren't there to escape any political strife, just the harsh, long winter chill back home. They came in the fall, and left in late spring—that was the routine. They'd been doing it for more than twenty years.

The head of the family was known as "Baba." Baba had two wives and four kids. They lived in a typical single-room farmhouse down the dirt road from our alleyway. Baba was a hardworking man who worked in the fields around the village to support his family. But sadly, this was not always enough to take care of his nomadic clan. To make ends meet, his two wives would take on odd jobs around the village. But after all of the years of coming and going, they were more than just seasonal travelers— they were considered family. The villagers would support them with food, wheat, clothing, and almost any kind of household item.

I hardly ever saw the younger of the two co-wives, but the oldest seemed to have a special place in everyone's heart. They looked to her as a divine healer of sorts. I found this out within my first few months in my new home.

***

I'm lying inside my mother-in-law's room on one of the wooden cots. My body's shivering with fever under a homemade padded comforter. The comforter is musty, as if it's not seen fresh air in years, but its heaviness is rather comforting to my aching body.

Hours seem to be dragging by. *Tick. Tick. Tick.* I can hear the clock across the room from time to time. Without TV or radio, I choose to entertain myself by studying the delicate details of the embroidered runner—orange, with yellow flowers—hung along the length of the wall-to-wall cement shelf. Next to my head, I see hair-like particles creeping out of the wall, lifting chunks of pastel-colored limestone away from the bricks.

I can hear family discussions and noises shuffling about outside, which makes no difference to me anyway, because I still can't understand what they are saying—it sounds like they are simply arguing all of the time.

Suddenly, Amijon walks in with a strange old woman who I've never seen before. The old woman's traditional Afghani wrap lifts in the front and is sitting atop her head like a warrior headpiece. It's almost identical to Amijon's old-fashioned mustard wedding *burqa*; but this one is old and faded black. Her baggy disheveled clothes give no hint of her twiggy figure. The thick colorful hand-beaded choker dominates her neckline. She is frail and extremely wrinkled.

The woman cautiously follows Amijon over to the side of my bed. Her eyes are huge and buggy. She almost scares me. My husband stands at the door so that the sun is still shining on him. He announces to me that Amijon has called the old woman to come and pray for me to heal.

"Okay," I say stuck between apprehension and appreciation.

I'm still lying flat with the covers up to my ears. I don't feel like sitting up for my new visitor. Instead, the cryptic healer leans in closely to my face—strangely close. *Can't she pray from over there?* I wonder

She starts mumbling to herself as the rest of the room watches in silence. Of course, I can't understand anything that she's saying, but I can't help but notice her teeth seem unusually large—totally disproportionate for her mouth. As I stare at her lips stretching back and forth like a rubber band, her fragile arm suddenly reaches up and grabs at my bedding to expose my shoulders. Without any warning, she begins spitting on my face. *Thup! Thup! Thup!* Just like you'd do if you'd just eaten a peanut shell, and you were trying to get all of the disgusting little pieces out of your mouth.

"What the …?" I gasp in shock. I look at my husband and squeal, "She's spitting on me! Why is she spitting on me?"

"She's praying for you. She doesn't mean anything by it. That's how *she* does it," he calmly explains as he chews a slice of orange,

That was the first of many times that *toop-valli boo boo* (translation: the spitting aunti) would come over and pray for me and the kids; we were always ready to block the spitting part at the end of her prayers.

Going Solo

It'd only been three months with our new family in Kalu when Zain blindsided me with an announcement. He'd decided to return to the States—without the kids and me. We were going to stay behind in Kalu and live with his family. He'd then send money from there to support us. His explanation for the sudden change was that since he couldn't read or write Urdu, the national language, it would be difficult for him to find work in Pakistan. And even if he were able to find a job, it wouldn't have been enough to support everyone; after all—according to local custom—since his father had passed away, he was now responsible for his mother and siblings, too.

I realize that I look really stupid at this point in the story. Even as I write this, I'm thinking to myself, *"Didn't we think about all of this stuff out before we picked up and left for another country? Oh come on, Marsha! You could not have been that irresponsible!"* But sadly enough, I was.

Needless to say, I was in utter shock. Suddenly, I was left alone with the two kids in a new country. Not to mention that I'd only learned a few words by then like "bread" and "water." What in the world was I going to do? Going back to the hellhole of the States where David could harass me wasn't an option.

The day Zain left, I couldn't stop crying. I was deeply in love with him; but also felt deserted and scared. Nonetheless, I trusted him with all of my heart. Each day I would lie to myself and say, *"It's okay, Yasmine. He just went to the store. He'll be back soon."*

At night, I would fall sleep with one child on each side of me. Then in the morning, I would repeat the same lie to myself again: *"He went shopping. He'll be back soon."*

Eventually, I stopped lying to myself and adjusted pretty well to my surroundings. I'd actually taken quite a liking to my new country. Whether the reason was that I'd always had an adventurous streak in me—or that I adjusted out of desperation, knowing that I couldn't go and face David—I don't know. But whatever kept me going, it worked.

Zain's family treated me like a princess in the beginning. I didn't have to cook or do any domestic chores. But boredom quickly set in. Thus, my natural curiosity took over, and I began experimenting with little things around the house like using the twig-broom to sweep the dirt, blowing on the fire, and putting more cow dung on it to keep it aflame. I had a fresh sense of freedom. Each moment was a gift—the adventure of a lifetime. I was confident that I'd found my refuge. I felt happy and alive. To be honest, I was truly happy for the first time in my life. The kids were radiant; they had gobs of cousin-friends, they were learning the language every day with lightning speed, they were playing with goats and marbles, and making mud patties, and running in and out of the house as kids do. It was a child's paradise.

The next of many challenges, I faced was learning to wear the *chadur*, or "the sheet" as I dubbed it. It's the covering, or veiling, that women wear in the villages. Some are solid black; some have red dots or designs like giant paw prints over them. My personal favorite was a white sheet with pink crocheted flowers. I'd wear this whenever I went outside of the home. My problem was that I just couldn't wear it like all of the other women. I was used to wearing a two-piece covering, consisting of a scarf and a long trench coat. But my mother-in-law felt it was time that I started to look more like them.

So, I practiced each day by putting the sheet on and taking it off. Imagine for a moment that you're taking a sheet from a double bed, and you are wrapping and tucking it around you so skillfully that only your eyes are showing. No hair. No skin. No lips. Only your eyes. Complicated, right? It would be easier to simply put it over your head and cut out holes for eyes, like for a ghost costume, which is basically how the old-fashioned coverings, or *burqas*, were anyway. Amijon still had her *burqa* from her wedding and she let me try it on for size. It was mustard yellow with yellow embroidering. It was difficult to see through the material mesh that covered the eyes. When I put the *burqa* on, I felt intensively clandestine, almost disconnected from the world. It was like wearing a small parachute; the material was endless and stuffy. It also reeked of mothballs; she must have it locked up since Zain's birth.

Thankfully, through trial and error, I learned how to wear the sheet, although not perfectly. Sometimes I would end up with only one eye poking out; sometimes the wind would catch it, and it would slip backwards off my head altogether. Anyone could tell I was an amateur. I can't count the number of times I stepped on the hem of the sheet and tripped myself. And going to the bathroom with it on? Don't even go there!

Nevertheless, I can proudly say that even after all these years, I can still put it on the correct way. An exceptional skill for my resume!

***

Now on opposite ends of the world, Zain and I were now in a long distance relationship. He would call me on a regular basis about money, family matters, and sometimes to just chat about life on both ends of the line.

During that time in 1992, the landline phone was the only way to contact anyone in the States. America Online (AOL) had just gotten jumpstarted when I left Phoenix, so the term "Internet" was only a whisper I had heard once or twice on the *Rush Limbaugh Show*. We didn't have a phone at home, so I'd have to go to the nearest city to receive a call. My brother-in-law, Riaz, had a vegetable store with a phone upstairs. Zain had arranged that the first Saturday of each month I'd take a horse and buggy, or *tonga*, into town to receive a call from America. This is how one Saturday went.

***

The *tonga* ride is bumpy as usual, the green fields calm and relaxing, the rocking of the buggy almost hypnotizing. But even with this relaxing ambiance, I have a sense of elation. As much as I love Zain, today it is not his voice that I'm excited to hear, but my mother's. She'll call me at exactly one p.m. our time.

The commotion of the city increases with each stride of the horse. The rush swells. The blaring screeches of the buses are nearly deafening. Bike riders ring their bells as they swipe by unsuspecting pedestrians. Cars, vans, horses, goats, pushcarts by the dozens. The street is a melting pot of pure chaos. The motor fumes are invasive. One main road and no rules.

We arrive at Riaz's store, and I carefully get down off the back of the *tonga*. Because of my excitement, the cement bridge over the drain gutter doesn't seem so narrow today. I have a certain bounce in my step, which easily vaults me straight over it to the staircase. The steps are awkwardly deep and narrow. I grab the sides of my sheet and lift it level with my knees, so as not to trip again. The higher I climb, the more the smell of onions and burlap grows—almost overbearing. But the joy of speaking to my mother makes the onions the sweetest smell of endearment.

"What time is it?" I ask myself. It's only ten minutes until one. I sit anxiously on the side rail of the *munja* (bed) and wait. My nephew brings me tea from the nearest tea stall.

"Here, m*ommi*," he says, *mommi* meaning auntie to him.

"*Shuklia*," I say, thanking him with greater confidence than before. "But where's the phone?"

"I'll get it," he says in an assuring voice.

The noise outside the window continues—the busy street below, yelling and honking, this is all I hear. I keep looking at my watch, anxious that I may miss the call. My nephew brings up the government-issued white phone and sets it on a small wooden table in front of me. This bland phone has no special LED displays, only short black buttons. Regardless, I sigh with relief that the phone is finally here with me.

Suddenly, it rings. I quickly snatch the receiver.

"Hello?" I say softly but anxiously.

"Marsha?" says the voice I've loved since my conception.

"Mom… Hi… Can you hear me? How are you?"

"Sissie," she says with a touch of relief. "I'm fine. How are you?"

In an instant, all of the noise in the background evaporates. My mother's sweet voice rings through the line, piercing my heart with such extreme joy. She's my only link to the world that I left behind. A discarded world that I have to learn to live without.

Our time runs out even faster than my mind accepts. My heart screams in pain as I try to say goodbye. "I love you, Mom." The word "goodbye" sticks in my throat and refuses to come out.

"I love you too, Sissie." The crackling of her voice echoes the love of a mother holding back tears. The phone goes dead. My grip tightens on the receiver.

For a few minutes, I had actually believed I was back in Phoenix. Right there with my mom, watching her soaps, chatting about the latest family dramas. But reality is overwhelming. I bravely wipe away the tears that are now streaming down and salting my lips.

I hardly remember the ride back to the village. Depression has fallen over me like a shadow. The night falls, and as I lay with the two kids next to me, I hold them tight and quietly cry myself to sleep.

The Kitchen

The kitchen is the heartbeat of families around the world and the heartbeat of my fondest memories in Kalu. So many things in our lives take place in this one remarkable space like eating, chatting, educating, and decision-making. Indeed, Kalu was no different. While there, I learned that the kitchen was not just a place in the home, but a state of mind. Washing dishes, cooking, and fuel supplies were the daily tasks for every woman in every home. Whether the women were cooking for their own family, or cooking for the workers in the fields, there were always decisions to make, and enough work to go around for everyone; even the kids loved to help.

I have to admit that when I first got there, I felt like the kitchen was a bit primitive, but it quickly became one of my favorite places. I was in awe watching the women cook—learning something new every day. I also believe that it was during the simple daily kitchen and cooking activities when I absorbed most of the local language, and thankfully so.

Dishes were washed on the ground by the bathroom water pump. We'd sit on the ground on very short little stools, usually about three to six inches off the ground. My butt was too big and my knees weren't flexible enough to allow me to reach their regular stools, so Amijon bought me a wider and taller one. It was about ten inches high and twelve inches wide— just perfect for big-booty-me. It was like having training wheels on a bike. It gave me time to learn how to squat down—using new sets of muscles.

We didn't use sponges to clean the dishes. Instead, we used old worn-out socks. We'd rub a sock on a square bar of soap, and then generously dab or swipe it onto some sand that was either in a small can or just lying on the ground next to us. Then, with this soapy-sandy mix, we'd scrub the silver plates and pans until the soapiness turned gray—leaving the silver dish gleaming. Scrubbing like this would usually take some muscle power—something else I had to learn. The faucet couldn't reach the area where we were sitting, so we used buckets of water to rinse the dishes. As soon as the bucket was empty, we'd get up for some more water. (Whenever *I* would do the dishes, my pant legs and the front of my long shirt, or *kameez*, would be totally soaked by the time I was done. Not fun in the wintertime, for sure.) Then, once we'd washed the dishes, we returned them to the kitchen and put them in the window to dry.

(The actual newspaper clipping that I sent to my mother in 1992—to show her how women did dishes in Kalu.)

We often cooked with clay pots as per tradition. Once the pots were used over the fire, we washed them like the other dishes (but very carefully), and then smeared a fresh coat of clay around the bottoms. This process protected them from breaking from the open flame. While clay pots are heavy and fragile, the flavor that they give to the food is well worth the extra effort that goes into cleaning them.

The kitchen door was only about five feet tall. I'd thought it'd purposely been built like that since Amijon was only four feet tall, but in reality they had raised the level of the courtyard a foot to prevent flooding during the rainy seasons. That initiative worked, but they'd left the door at its original setting, thus making it too short. A perfect fit—if it were for Alice in Wonderland.

Meal preparations would sometimes begin at the crack of dawn, and prepping was not restricted to the kitchen. We'd clean and chop food anywhere around the home: on the bed, in the yard, upstairs on the roof. Usually, we'd choose the day's spot for preparation according to weather. In the summer, we would run from the sun, but in winter, we sought it out like heat-seeking missiles. However, regardless of weather, we still had to cook at the fireplace. No getting around that—summers were brutal.

Likewise, we'd knead the dough for the unleavened bread by squatting down on any flat surface in the yard or bedroom. We mixed the ingredients in a deep silver round dish, called a *thrammi*. Sometimes we'd have to knead the dough two or three times a day, depending on how many people there were to cook for. Making dough was exhaustingly hard for me to learn. But luckily, my mother-in-law was extremely patient. I messed up so many times, either by mixing in too much water, or not getting the salt just right, but she persisted. I finally got it down pat. Yet another astonishing skill for my resume!

(Amijon kneading the dough in front of the kitchen.)

Since Kalu is a farming community, most of the women prepare meals not only for their own children and family members, but also for the men working in the fields. Each day was different; there would be anywhere from ten to thirty men to cook for at one lunch setting. Catering for a husband who runs farmland is a full-time job in itself.

The cuisine in Kalu is simply amazing and fresh. The most popular dish is a type of stew, or *salan* (for lack of a better way to explain it). All of the ingredients are cooked in a single, bowl-shaped clay pot on an open fireplace—either in or outside the kitchen. Twigs, chopped wood, and dried cow dung patties fuel the fire. I became very skilled in starting fires with cow poop, kerosene, a plastic bag and a single match. Okay, I admit: there were times on windy days when I had to use two or three matches, but I did it. *And* I burnt my eyes about a million times puffing on the flames. *Ouch!*

Even so, I feel very blessed to have learned this cooking method and other ways to cook tasty, authentic Pakistani food from my mother-in-law. Even Gordon Ramsay would be jealous of the hands-on knowledge that I've gained. I learned to clean, cut, and even how to seed food. I *still* cook the dishes I learned from Kalu on a regular basis. The scents of Pakistani and Indian spices are my catnip.

Another amazing feat is that I learned how to cut meat into little pieces without the use of a cutting board. I can use a knife and one foot to do it. Honestly, it was a blast learning how to do this. It's really simple—I sit on the small stool, hold the knife with my toes, while leaning the blade up against a wall for leverage—this leaves me with two free hands to cut the meat as needed. Quite ingenious, really!

We cooked bread, or *roti* in yet another section of the yard. It was usually baked in an igloo-shaped clay oven built from an old steel barrel and then attached with mud-paste directly to a connecting wall. Women then gather twigs, branches and leaves from nearby fields in order to heat it for baking. Even though the actual chore of baking in these ovens is extremely hot, women often choose this method in order to save time. They could cook all of the bread needed for the family in one *heating*-session. And just in case you were wondering, the rubric used for determining how much bread to cook was one man equals two oven-baked *rotis*.

Sometimes, we only needed to prepare few pieces of bread. In that case, we would use a griddle on the same fire that we were cooking the dinner's stew. And if unexpected company came over, then we got to use the gas cylinder. *Yay!*

Still, despite finding myself mesmerized by the food and the methods of cooking it, this unorganized style of going to and fro freaked me out.

Every time we cooked, I couldn't help but think, *"There has to be a better way."* I soon felt it was my calling in life to overhaul this kitchen nightmare completely. It took me a while, but I eventually had a modern kitchen built for us including a fireplace, a dishwashing area and running water –all in one room. It was amazing—we could cook, clean and sit for a cup of tea—without setting foot outside. We still did dishes on the ground inside the kitchen, but I had to take baby steps with change. The only thing left outdoors was the baking of bread in the main oven. I just couldn't figure that one out. *Cursed smoke!*

(Me and Roni, having some fun. Around 1992.)

As if bringing all of these things together wasn't enough, I also presented another refreshing concept to the kitchen—decorating. I started with curtains and a fresh paint job. What an American thing to do, right? My new sister-in-law Roni (who by the way quickly became my new best friend and mentor by teaching me the Hindko language and everything village-domestic) really loved the new ideas and accepted everything with great fervor. We both enjoyed the new American styling; but I too accepted change. I particularly fell in love with the open cement shelving style that was common. This introduced me to the joy of not having kitchen cabinets. Even in my home today, I have taken down all of the cupboard doors. I have to look at all of my dishes in the open. Truly, it's a conditioned response.

***

Whenever I talk about Kalu and the kitchen, I can't help but remember a couple of my favorite cooking stories.

Roni is cooking for the men in the field—as she does every day. I've only been in Pakistan about six months, and I still have no solid language skills. I know a few things, but I still can't speak up quickly enough when needed. On this particular day, Roni is cooking meat *salan*—small pieces of cow meat, onions, tomatoes, ginger and garlic, along with the accompanying spices. As usual, we're cooking on the normal mud-coated fireplace outside, behind the kitchen, using firewood from our own trees on the farm, and cow dung patties.

Lunch is usually ready around eleven-thirty, so we've started first thing this morning to make sure that it's ready on time. It's about nine-ish, and we've just made the tea for the men in the field for their morning tea break. One of my brothers-in-law comes home to pick up the tea. As is his habit, he inspects whatever is cooking for the day. I'm standing about fifteen feet away, not really interested in what he's doing because I've seen him do it a hundred times already. I watch him as he leans over the fireplace and removes the lid of the clay pot. Instead of leaning the lid against the back wall behind the pot, he lays it down flat on the firewood—wet-side down.

He picks up the handmade wooden ladle and stirs the pot, inspecting it, and with a gesture of acceptance, he grabs the lid from the firewood to put it back on the pot. As he is lifting the lid, I see something brown and fuzzy stuck to the bottom. Of course, it doesn't dawn on him that the bottom of the lid is wet with the steam of the stew. Lo and behold, there is a piece of cow poop stuck to the bottom. Before I can think of the words to tell him to stop, he places the lid back on the pot. I silently gasp and cringe while I scrunch my face. He is oblivious to what he has done and walks away.

I stand there in shock of what I just saw. I run over to the pot to see if it I can get the cow poop out of the stew. But when I lift the lid, there's nothing there. It's already gone into the water. Hanging my head in disappointment, I think about what I can do now. I don't know how to tell them that there is cow poop in the pot. They wouldn't understand me for sure; they'll think that I have gone crazy again, like the time Shedi was crying for a cucumber and they couldn't understand me. *Just leave it; I guess there's nothing that I can do.* Instead, I decide just to cook something else for the kids and me.

So, I calmly go to the kitchen and sauté some tomatoes and onions. When it comes time for lunch, Amijon tries to give me some of the cow poop salan—or better known with my kids as the *cow poop cultivy* (The word *cultivy* is the Hinko name for the clay pot, which is used to cook the stew.) "Oh, no, thank you," I say with a smile on my face, shaking my palm as politely as possible. "Not today."

The rest of the day, I sing a little song I created with the dandiest country-western twang that I can conjure up.

Cow poop cultivy, cow poop cultivy.
It's the best cow poop in town <upward-twang>!
Cow poop cultivy, cow poop cultivy.
It's the greatest cow poop in town <downward-twang>!

That night, I taught the kids a new mom-made nursery rhyme. And to this day, I still kick into it whenever I'm reminded of the cow poop cultivy story.

***

Another funny story took place about five years after the cultivy incident.

I was living in my own home across the alleyway from my mother-in-law's house. It was a national holiday, and I'd left that morning to visit some friends around the village. I'd had a delightful time but I was getting tired and couldn't wait to get home to rest. It was about five in the afternoon when I walked in and stopped dead in my tracks—I couldn't believe my eyes. There was a butchered cow piled up in the center of my living room. An oozing mountain of freshly cubed cow meat—lying on a sheet in the middle of the room—an entire bull. I nearly had a heart attack.

"Whaaat is this!? Why is this in my house?" I screamed.

Amijon came from out of the kitchen and without hesitation replied, "Oh, I didn't have the room at my house, so I put it here—in yours."

You can just imagine my shock and horror. My house had become the command center for meat distribution. Apparently, they were passing out the meat to people in the village as an act of charity. That was great, but I had an unpolished cement floor in my living room and there was only a cotton sheet between the floor and the mountain of oozing cow—that meant that blood went into every one of those tiny holes in the floor. *How gross!*

No matter how many times I scrubbed the floor, I could smell that bloody bull for weeks.

(Mona, playing dress up with my chadur. 1992)

Drive-Up Munja Night

You might be thinking that I must have gotten pretty bored in the village. I admit there were times when I was bored out of my mind. But I found things to keep me busy. I learned to sew; I studied the native languages, Urdu, Punjabi, Hindko and a touch of Pushto (by the way, I can still write in Urdu up to the third grade level); and I learned how to survive harsh winters without heaters, and steaming summers without AC. Nevertheless, admittedly, there were times when I would literally prowl around the yard looking for something to entertain me.

Until one day in late 1992, while rummaging through my clothes and stuff, I ran upon my mother's paperback dictionary that she had given me while I was packing to leave the States. It was a set—a*Webster's*

Dictionary with an accompanying thesaurus. Each was the size of a regular paperback novel, just shy of two inches thick.

Those days, we only had a small, black and white twelve-inch TV. With very little English programming, I wasn't drawn to it too much (but more about that later), and for reading, the only thing I had at the time was a newspaper that one of my brothers-in-law would bring for me about twice a month. (With that I was easily able to follow the Chess World Championship saga that Garry Kimovich Kasparov won again. The rest of the news in it was boring political drama that I wasn't interested in.)

So, finding the dictionary was quite a treat for me. With my newfound entertainment, I'd sit anywhere for hours in the sun and begin reading down the list of words it as if it were a story. I'd never seriously studied words and their history before, so this new-found knowledge absolutely fascinated me. The dictionary took on an angelic form to me—a refuge, if you will—and I started practicing the pronunciations and spellings aloud. My family thought I was crazy.

It was during this time that I fell in love with the English language—deeply madly truly. Each word was a complete sentence in itself; each had a personality, a family, and a history. I'd sit and ponder a single word for hours. I'm really ashamed that it took leaving my own country to explore and learn about my own language.

Since then, I've acquired an extensive collection of dictionaries in my home. A strange feeling overcomes me when I hold one in my hands. A chill almost goes through me; it's very difficult to explain. And of course, I still have my mother's little blue dictionary sitting on my shelf today. I love that little blue book. It's now yellowed with age and bears witness to the years of being in pocket. Before my mother passed away, she sent me her diamond earrings that I'd once given her for her birthday, but these earrings are not the most precious things that I have from her. Instead, it's this *Webster's* set, and the love for language that she sparked within me.

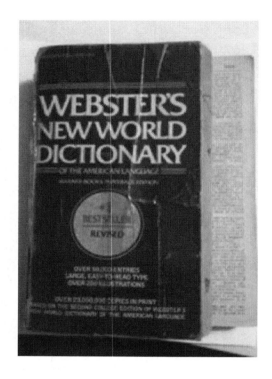

(My little blue dictionary that my mother gave me. 2016)

All in all, TV did have *some* presence in my life. The only English shows I can remember watching were *Knight Rider* and *Are You Being Served?* However, Thursday nights turned out to be my favorite night for TV. The only channel at that time, PTV, would feature a popular Pakistani movie each Thursday night. This event was a huge hit in the village. Family from all across the village would come over to our house to watch the Thursday Night Movie. (Very few homes had TV sets at the time.)

During the summer nights, we'd lie outside on *munjas*, or twin-sized portable cots, and watch the movie together.

The weekly event was so enjoyable that I nicknamed it—*drive-up munja night*. It reminded me of the old Thunderbird drive-in movies back home in Phoenix. But instead of the back of the pickup truck, we had the munja. And instead of the big screen, we had the little black and white TV.

To set the mood for each Thursday night, we'd set the TV on a small wooden table outside Amijon's room, just as far as the electrical cord would allow. On each side of the TV, we'd place two oscillating stand-up fans, these too with the electric cords pulled as far as they could reach. We'd strategically place the *munjas* all over the courtyard so everyone would get a good view of the television. Some of the neighbors would even bring their own beds, so the yard got full pretty quickly. It was a weekly mini-family reunion—with aunts, uncles, and kids alike.

After sunset, the yard would start bubbling with anticipation of the upcoming movie. Chatter about the day's events filled the air. But once the movie started, no one dared speak a word. It was dead silent among the viewers. All you could hear was the movie's dramatic overacting that shot out of the little magical box between the two fans. But during commercials, the crowds went crazy discussing the storyline—which was usually some sappy love drama where boy meets girl, girl can't marry boy because her father won't let her, boy says he will die without her, *blah, blah, blah*. Because I couldn't understand the language very well, I'd spent a good amount of the time just lying on my back, staring out into space. Less light pollution in the countryside meant *awesome* star gazing for me. It was the first time that I'd had a chance to see the Milky Way. It was breathtaking.

Overacting aside, it was a delightful way to spend each Thursday night. The colorful outfits and the music hypnotized me. I'll never forget the night we stayed up late to watch Adnan Sami's "*Sargam*" in 1995. (Amazing music! The soundtrack from that movie is still one of my all-time favorite albums.)

Summers were especially good because, once the movie was over, we'd arrange the beds horizontally in a long line, directly in front of one of the stand-up oscillating fans. Your hierarchy in the family determined your position in the bed line. The kids and I would get the first bed right in front of the fan, because I was still determined a visitor, allowing us to get the most air. My brothers-in-law would get the next three beds because they were the breadwinners of the family. Next would be any visiting cousins or aunts, then my mother-in-law, and then finally, at the very end, Roni. I really felt bad for her. Not only did she have the crappiest munja in the home, but also the air was nothing but a whisper by the time it reached her. She'd have to cover herself with a sheet each night to protect against mosquitoes. Amazingly, she never complained. Nonetheless she was vindicated when the electricity would go out, because then *we* were ones fighting the army of mosquitoes; and we weren't so used to it like she was. While the rest of us were scratching from bug bites, she was sound asleep.

Knock Knock

Of all the words in the Hindko language, the word that stands out as the most annoying to me is the word *mezman*. I heard that bloody word so much that whenever I heard it, I'd cringe and my stomach would literally hurt. *Mezman*'s actual definition means *"guests, or visitors,"* but my twisted translation of this word means: *"Yasmine, people are here to look at you again."*

For me, *mezman* meant torment—I was just so sick and tired of people coming over to look at me—all because white American women in Kalu were a very rare event. I know down deep that they meant no harm, but it was still so exasperating.

That aside, I found it quite interesting how the villagers treated company—other members of the family and outsiders alike. There was a certain unspoken etiquette to follow whenever company came over. These rules covered topics, like how to greet guests, how to seat them, how to serve tea, and how to present meals. Middle Eastern cultures have it down to a science.

For example, black tea mixed with milk is a huge part of the village culture. You have to make tea for anyone that comes over to visit you. If you don't offer tea, you're surely going to insult that visitor. And vice-versa, if the visitor doesn't drink the tea, then the host is offended. Just presenting the tea to guests had certain intimidating guidelines. Learning all of them was sometimes very daunting, but at times quite comical. A typical scene would play out for me like this.

A string of veiled women nonchalantly enters the front gate of our courtyard. A heavy-set elderly woman is leading the pack. Her green veiling is pulled up on each side and resting proudly on her shoulders. Her hair and hands are bright orange with henna. I've been here for a year now, so this scene is all too familiar.

"Begum?" she bellows, swaying back and forth like a pregnant woman in her final trimester. "Where are you?"

"Oh, you came?" Amijon replies as she emerges out of her bedroom and into the courtyard.

The greeting ritual begins. The typical greeting between two women starts with an embrace, touching their head once to the right shoulder, then to the left, then back to the right. The elder of two then kisses the cheeks or forehead of the other woman as a sign of affection before ending with a handshake as the two pull apart. This same ritual continues through the line of visitors with each woman of the household. Depending on how many women are present, this could take up to twenty minutes to complete. (Weddings are notorious for lengthy greetings.) Today's visitors have all have come to look at the *godi*, Yasmine. My aunt doesn't mind if they tag along, because after all, she gets to show off her American niece.

"Come on in," Amijon continues while leading them into her room. The line of women happily file in.

One by one, Amijon gives a friendly tug at their veils. "Take it off! Take it off!" she encourages. "Make yourselves at home. Put your feet up. This is your home."

She then turns to her sister and the next step of the ritual begins. "Oh, so nice to see you," Amijon starts. "How are you? How have you been?"

"Oh sister, I've been okay. I've been to the doctor three times this week. Don't know what is happening with my knee."

"How is your son, Ahmed?" Amijon continues.

"He is fine."

"How is your daughter-in-law, Maria?"

"She's fine."

"How is your other son, Mobi?" The list of names must continue as my mother-in-law is obligated to name all of her nieces and nephews one-by-one, so as not to offend her sister.

"He is fine too, sister," she says. This play of back and forth continues for ten minutes. Finally, the tide reverses and it is now the other's turn to repeat the same line of questioning. (You have to see this in action to believe it. I lost my patience with this custom early on and just started asking visitors, "How is everyone?")

Meanwhile, I've already gotten bored by this repeated line of questioning and have escaped to prepare the tea with our finest china. Because it is for *mezman*, I'm allowed to use the gas stove instead of the firewood. *Yay!*

All is ready. A full thermos of steaming chai—tea mixed with milk and sugar—and a little plate of the round almond cookies from the neighborhood family store. I'm so proud of myself—I've prepared the serving tray just right. I hope. I firmly grip the two handles and begin my approach into Amijon's bedroom to serve the visiting judges.

Amijon swells with pride, as the visitors peer at the white daughter-in-law, so obediently serving the guests. Eyes peer and snickers are exchanged, as I stay focused on my task at hand — in order to not flub up again. These women cannot wait to get home and tell their families that the Kalu white girl served them tea and cookies.

I place the tray down on the small awkward coffee table, set up the teacups with their matched saucers and begin pouring. "Chai pi say? (Would you like some tea to drink?)" I ask, knowing that they will all get a good laugh out of it. They do. Unfortunately, I don't fill one of the cups enough—the tea has not reached the rim of the cup. My mother-in-law jumps up to rescue the day. Her eyes go from laughter and pride to a scowl in an instant like a mother cat correcting her young.

"Koltyni thee! (You donkey's daughter!) You have to fill it to the rim of the cup! How many times do I have to tell you that?" she abruptly instructs. The visitor's eyes pop open.

I just snicker shyly and say, "Oops! Teek hai. (Okay.)," before pouring the rest of the cups, making sure to have filled them to the rim this time. Amijon returns to her seat, mumbling more obscenities under her breath.

My aunt, smirking, leans in closer to me and asks, "Yasmine, doesn't it make you mad that she calls you names like that?"

I look up at my aunt with a huge smile on my face. Then reply with genuine acceptance, "Oh no, not at all. 'Donkey's daughter' is my mother-in-law's pet name for me. I love her like my mother. She can call me that all she wants. It doesn't bother *me*."

The room erupts in laughter. My mother-in-law's scorn has turned to delight. She laughs too. (You see, I realized early on that the Hindko language is a very rough language; so I know she meant nothing bad by calling me those names—it was just her culture talking. Sometimes just for fun, I'll mimic Amijon's accent and call my daughter '*Koltyni thee*'. We giggle every time.)

Cow Patties

Cows are an extremely vital part of everyday lives in the village—providing milk, meat, and fuel for the fire. To have a storage room full of dry cow patties is a dream come true for some women I know. I, myself, have bought a couple potato sacks full of them for around one Rupee each.

Throughout the day, women take piles of fresh cow dung from the cow's area and set it aside for later use. Then, each morning they collect and mix these piles with straw and some water—by hand. Once the dung is mixed, they form the dung into a desired shape and set in the sun to dry. The resulting patties are then shaped according different to drying techniques.

If there's limited sun, then the patties are hand-splattered on the sunny side of the house or wall, but if there's easy access to a rooftop, then the typical gumdrop-shape works better. In any case, once dry, they're stored in a dry place—and *voila*—you have kindling. It's lightweight as compared to actual wood, and it is very rough to the touch. It also has a fuzzy appearance because pieces of straw are sticking out all around it.

These patties work best for starting fires for cooking. We'd break off a huge chunk of a patty, pour some kerosene oil all over it, and light with a match—works every time. They're also useful for keeping the fire going if there was a shortage of firewood.

Another great thing that I learned about cow dung is that once it burns there's lots of useful ash left behind. We'd save it for several odd uses around the home. My personal favorite was using it to clean up baby diarrhea that fell on the ground. We'd flatten down the ash bricks, take it over to the spot where the baby had pooped, shake the desired amount of ash on it, sweep it up again, and then just throw it away. (I would have never thought of *that* in a million years. Cow poop helps clean up baby poop. What an amazing circle of life.)

Still, despite my fascination with cow patties, only once during my entire stay in Pakistan did I make gumdrop cow patties on the roof of my mother-in-law's home. It was an unusual adventure for sure. It reminded me of mixing meatloaf, but much smellier. And yes, I had a huge audience cheering me on while doing so. One time was enough for *me*, though. It took me several washings to get it out from under my fingernails. *Yuck!*

Am I Dying?

One day, I thought I was dying. No really. I honestly thought I was dying. It was 1992, and I was on my period sitting in the black bathroom. I looked down on my pad, and saw about eight little white worms squirming around. "What?" I gasped in disbelief. I began crying right there in the bathroom. Zain was not in Pakistan at the time, so I had no one to talk to about it. I was totally alone and scared. I can still see the worms now.

***

The bathroom is dark—somehow, even darker than before. Tears are streaming down my face. *What's happening with me?* My mind races a thousand different directions. *Oh my God, am I dying? Are these worms eating me on the inside? Of course they are; they're eating something. They're eating me! What am I gonna do? There's no doctor in this stupid town.*

I stand up, still sobbing. I pull myself together enough to step out of the bathroom and go into Amijon's room. "I have to talk to Zain," I say to myself. "He'll know what I should do. Oh man, I can't even call him myself. Okay. I'll just have to wait until someone comes home so they can call him."

Minutes crawl by at a snail's pace. I decide pacing is better than sitting. I look over at the useless white phone on top of the fridge. "What good is having a stupid phone if you can't call *out* on it?" I yell at the phone, as if expecting it to answer me. My pacing becomes tenser as the minutes go by. I throw my hands in the air and bellow, "Oh my god, where are they? These worms are eating me right now. They're in my stomach. I'm gonna die! Oh my God! They've got to be able to do something." Then a sobering thought hits me and I weaken to a whisper. "Maybe it's too late."

I am on the verge of going crazy. My heart and breathing pulsate. Finally, one of the brothers comes home, and I demand to call America immediately. "I have to call right now!" My words jump out at him without any control of my own.

He assures me that he will go to the nearest city, put out a call to Zain and have him call me here at home.

Two hours go by. I am numb from worry. Suddenly, the phone rings. I answer as quickly as it emits sound. "Zain! What took you so long!?" He babbles on about something, but I refuse to listen and just cut him off mid-sentence. "Never mind that! I have to go to the doctor's right now. I just found worms on my pad. They're probably eating me alive right now—as we're speaking. Tell your brother to take me to the doctor in Kamra right now."

I hand the phone to the brother who has slipped into the room to obviously eavesdrop. Zain instructs him to get a car and take me to the Kamra Military Base Hospital.

We fetch a car and again time seems to be crawling. We arrive at the hospital check post. The driver goes into the small room to submit his papers. He seems to take forever before he finally returns and we begin our journey around the winding roads of the base. We pull up to the women's section of the hospital and I quickly go into a waiting room where I join about thirty other women ahead of me. It doesn't matter how many at this point, because I am already so completely exasperated. Amijon is with me and gets my name on the register. We sit and wait. My heart leaps with each opening of the doctor's door. They call my name.

I go into a cold brown office—not a hospital room, an office. The doctor is in her late 40s, slightly overweight and wearing a *sari* military uniform (a long wrap-style garment that flows to the floor and drapes over one shoulder). I notice that her nametag says "Yasmine."

"How can I help you today?" she asks.

"Thank God you speak English," I spew out. "You have to help me."

"What's wrong?" she says.

"I'm on my period and I found about eight little white worms on my pad," I say, while demonstrating their size with my thumb and index finger.

The doctor listens and says, "Okay. Let's take a look."

My heart is racing and my knees are weak. I am so humiliated for her to see me in this condition. The anxiety is nearly more than I can bear. All I keep thinking about is the white demons eating my body and that every minute that goes by is wasted.

I lay on the cold, padded surface, praying for God to help me.

"So, where are you from, England or America?" She asks while examining me.

"America." I sputter, trying not to be annoyed at her useless small talk.

Finally, the doctor straightens up and says, "Yes, you're right. You do have worms. But they're not coming from where *you* are thinking. They are coming from your intestines."

"What?" I bark out. "Are you serious? Oh, that's disgusting! How did I get worms?"

"Probably from the food you're eating. Not to worry. This is common this time of year, or whenever we eat a lot of stuff made with garbanzo bean flour. I'll prescribe some medicine for you, and that'll clear them right up." She continues—apparently thinking I need more of an explanation of this wormy-phenomenon, "The reason that you're seeing them on your pad is because they are coming outward to lay their eggs."

My eyebrows pop upward in shock. *What?*

She continues without missing a beat, "You'll usually feel an itching sensation. This is because they are biting tiny holes to put their eggs in—around the anus." Her demonstration is nearly obscene. "Have you been itching lately?"

My jaw drops open. *Am I really having this conversation right now?* I manage to answer her in a bland drawn-out voice, "No-o. I don't think so-o."

"Well, anyway," she says nonchalantly, "you should take this medicine every six months just to clear any worms that you may get later."

Get later? Again? Oh, crap! I quickly ask, "Should I give it to my kids, too?"

"Yes. You can. The whole family should take one tablet every six months for preventative measures."

I left the hospital that day *very* relieved that I was not dying. We immediately got the medicine, and I passed it out as if it were candy. Needless to say, the kids and I took that *butt-medicine* every six months like clockwork—just to make sure! It was then that I really understood why Zain taught me to say *"Medi tooee krudik onihae."* (My butt itches.)

(My first time milking the cow.)

Animal Kingdom

Worms weren't the only creatures that we encountered in Pakistan. The kids and I had a wonderful time experiencing *all* that nature had to offer: bugs, snakes, spiders, unusually big ants, bats, beetles, termites, wasps, crows, goats, slugs, and lots and lots of cockroaches. I learned so much more about the animal kingdom, than I ever knew before. For instance, cows are emotional creatures; they cry for the ones they love. I saw our cow cry out several times for Amijon when she would leave the courtyard to go do something. Cows also use their tails to slap anything that may be irritating them—humans included. I found that out the hard way a couple of times. (By the way Bessie, I'm still mad about that time you slapped me upside the face. I was trying my best to milk you the correct way. Really, I was.)

Do you remember as a kid seeing those swarms of bees in cartoons? Well, that is really how they interact. On two different occasions, I saw swarms flying overhead while I was working on the roof of my home. The first time, I was hanging up some laundry when I heard a buzzing sound in the distance. I scanned the sky and saw a huge swarm headed my way. I froze. At first, I was in awe of them, until it dawned on me that they were heading in my direction and I could very well be attacked. Thankfully, they flew right over my head and swooped down into a woodpile on the next-door neighbor's roof. Scary stuff. The buzzing was *so* intense.

And did you know that rabbits can scream? One time while I was really bored, I decided to teach the kids how to catch the two rabbits that we had in the courtyard. We set up the old-fashioned trick box—an old wooden crate propped up with a stick—with some grass in it as bait. We tied a string to the stick, and hid around the corner and waited. As soon as the rabbit came for the bait, down came the box. *BLAM!* It was ours. We were so excited. I ran to the box, reached in, and grabbed the rabbit by its leg. The rabbit screamed at me. *What the...?* It startled me so badly that I let go.

(Our rabbits.)

The most amazing animal that we interacted with in Pakistan was a baby sparrow that we raised. My son (who was around nine at the time) brought the baby home; she'd fallen out of her nest. The bird didn't even have its feathers yet and had lost its mother. So, we decided to go ahead and take care of it ourselves. She was so small that I was afraid she wasn't going to make it. I mixed some flour and water together and tried to get her to take some from a syringe. It didn't work.

Later, while I was trying to feed the bird again, my son popped out from behind the table, flapping his arms and squawking. "Chae chae," he squawked like a baby bird.

"What are you doing?" I snapped. It really was the most ridiculous thing to see. But can you believe that the baby bird opened her mouth like she wanted food? Taking advantage of my son's experiment, I hurried and dropped some of the mixture in. Shedi jumped and squawked again. The bird opened again. This went on for days. By and by, the bird started opening her mouth whenever we waved the syringe in a circular motion above her head. It was an amazing thing to watch.

We named our new pet, Jewel. Jewel gained weight quickly and her feathers came in nicely. She grew to love the flour mixture and other vegetables; even waking me up when it was time for her to eat. Interestingly enough, we helped her wings get stronger by having her sit on a stick, and bouncing it slowly in midair. This exercise developed her flapping technique quite well. We were so excited the first time she took off and flew around the house. She became a very beloved part of the family.

Jewel had free reign of the home and would fly to her heart's content. One day she flew out an open door by mistake. Both of the kids started crying. We thought we had lost her for good, but it turned out she wasn't far. We could hear and see her on the roof next door. I held her syringe up and did the squawking feeding noise, thinking that by some slim chance it might draw her attention in. It did. She came back in the door. We were ecstatic. She was now with us because she wanted to be. She then had free reign of the house *and* the world outside. Just like a pet, we let her out to roam and then she would come to the door and squawk at us to let her in. Yep. Jewel was pretty amazing.

(I'm wearing my favorite white chadur while Shedi gets
to control the tonga.)

The Tonga

During the first fourteen years I was in Pakistan, I didn't personally
own a car. Instead, we rode the horse and buggy, or *tonga*, all the time
around the villages. Driving in that country was extremely dangerous and
terrifying, so I really wasn't in big hurry to drive anyway. But, oh, how
I loved the *tonga*! There was something about the *tonga*'s earthiness and
serenity that brought me such peace. Come. Let's take a ride.

***

Today, Amijon and I are taking the *tonga* to go shopping in *Hazro's meena bazaar*, the nearest shopping market, for some material to have some clothes sewn up for the kids. The *tonga's* waiting for us outside at the end of the alleyway. It's a one-horse-drawn buggy with only two wheels. The horse is white and brown and a bit undernourished— his hipbones far too obvious, with open wounds to boot. The curved canopy atop the buggy is a dirty brown and decorated with red flower-shaped leather pieces—about the size of quarters—tacked along the edges. Its supporting wood has darkened with age, and huge tears in all directions echo the years of past service. It covers just enough of the sun to get by.

There are two sets of seats for passengers. Because I'm not experienced enough to ride in the back, my mother-in-law puts me in the front. You see, to ride in the back of the buggy, you need to hold on with one hand, and balance yourself with your feet pressing firmly against the foot bar at the bottom. This gives you the leverage that you need to support yourself when you hit the bumps in the roads. If you don't hold on correctly, then you'll fall off. So, since I'm the virgin rider, the kids and I are told to get up front today.

We do as instructed. The driver doesn't speak a word to me. He's very respectful and stands up to allow the kids and me to sit down. As we start our journey, the creaking of the old wood sounds like the wheels are in pain as they follow the niches of the dirt road. Once we reach the long stretch of the paved road leading into town, the *tonga* moves steadily, bobbing rhythmically. It sounds like music. *Tuck, tuck, tuck, tuck* rings out as the horse's hoofs hit the asphalt. The rhythm changes with speed.

The refreshing scent of the pastures lingers in my nostrils: field after field of greenery, with rows meticulously carved out for watering. We see women along the fields walking opposite us, carrying stuffed cloth shopping bags on their heads as they are returning from the market; perhaps they cannot afford a *tonga* ride, thus enduring the long walk home. I can see the city in the distance. Motorcycles zoom past so fast it's as if we're standing still. The horse suddenly shakes his head with a snort, and slobber shoots off the sides of the bridle.

I'm enjoying this ride tremendously. It's like a dream—peaceful and serene. That is until the horse lifts his tail. Slowly the long tail lifts upward in the air. Without warning—and without missing a beat—he begins pooping right in front of us while trotting. (Now that's talent, ladies and gentlemen.) Luckily, our front seat puts us about six inches above the tail, but it still gives us an unwelcome front-row view. My eyes are as big as silver dollars, but the kids let out a squeal. They think that this is the funniest thing they've ever seen. They're pointing and laughing. Well, at least it isn't diarrhea (now that's another story for another time). Still, my first ride is forever imprinted on my heart.

I can see the city in the distance, trotting closer with each strike of the hoof. The traffic is also getting denser. I notice that *tongas* vary in color and design. It appears to be the same with the trucks, too. Many of these vehicles are decorated with bright-colored plastic flowers and painted pictures of Bollywood divas.

It's also getting extremely loud. As we merge into traffic, the cars are honking profusely, and I hear men barking out things I don't understand. I start to feel a bit of anxiety. A whole lot of noise and a whole lot of color—total chaos. This entry into the city is nothing like the pleasant ride we had coming in. The contrast is deafening.

***

Eventually, I graduated to sitting in the back of the *tonga*, but it took some practice. To get up on the backseat was a bit trickier than the front.

For instance, you have to securely hold your veil with one hand, and then grasp the wooden frame of the canopy *tightly* with the free hand. Once you're confident, you place your foot on the mounting step and hop up—while twirling counterclockwise—plopping down on the seat. It took me a while before I mastered this method. A *long* while.

The biggest thing to watch out for while riding on the back of the *tonga* were the bloody bumps in the roads. Oftentimes, you're holding on to the frame good enough with your one hand, you're placing your foot on the foot bar like you're supposed to—with just the right pressure—and then suddenly, *thunk*, you hit a bump in the road, which causes the buggy to violently jerk to and fro. Then, *blam!* You just hit your head on the canopy.

But there's hope. If your canopy-holding arm is loose enough, it will act as a shock absorber; then, hopefully, you won't have a bump on your head, after the bump on the road. This is yet another lesson learned the hard way. It happened to me more than once. It gives a whole new meaning to *school of hard knocks*, for sure.

When I first arrived in Kalu, these traditional *tongas* were, by far, the cheapest and most popular form of transportation. But about ten years later, things started changing. Boisterous and suffocating rickshaws were replacing *tongas*. Plus, eventually cars and motorcycles started overshadowing even the most poorest of villages.

It has been many years since my ride in Kalu, but I still yearn for that soothing musical wobble of the beloved, historic *tonga*.

Laundry

There were countless new things to learn in the village. But I have to say, the hardest thing to get used to was laundry. Gone were the days I'd just put the dirty clothes in the wash machine, add detergent, and push the button. Now I had to start a fire to heat the soap and water, cut a bar of soap into small workable pieces, wait for it to dissolve, sit on the ground in front of shallow wash pans, and hand-wash the clothes. Then, I'd hand-pump the water into a bucket to rinse the clothes, ring them out, pump water again, rinse again, and then hang them to dry. Every single piece of laundry was done separately. Imagine doing this for twelve people in the family! I remember several times, seeing Amijon start the laundry at the crack of dawn, and still be working on it late into the evening. She and Roni would actually have to tag-team it to get it done. In the winter, laundry work would often bleed over into two washing days—the amount of clothing worn doubled.

And the spring cleaning days were murder. Sheets and duvet covers galore to be washed by hand—oh man, I get shivers when I think about the amount of time and effort that we put into it. Summertime was generally easier in the sense that clothes dried fairly quickly in the open sunlight— that was a plus. But winter was brutal. Thankfully, the climate in Kalu was almost identical to Phoenix; even so, it would still take sometimes up to three or four days for a single sweater to dry.

When I first arrived in Kalu, I was oblivious to the amount of work involved with doing laundry by hand. The only time I ever remember washing anything out by hand was during a camping trip when I had to wash out a pair of my jeans; I was about fifteen years old, and really a dork.

I somehow got the birdbrain idea to use a rock to bang some spot out, and I ended up making a hole instead.

Anyway, it wasn't until later that first year in 1992, when Amijon insisted that I start washing my own laundry by hand, that I realized a couple of different things about life. Number one: Clothes are not as dirty as we first think they are. *Hmm, yeah, I can wear this one more day.* Number two: I needed a washing machine—ASAP.

As you can probably guess, it wasn't too long after my epiphany that we got a washing machine for the house; I feel really ashamed that it took my hands to ache before I realized how sore Amijon's were all along. The washing machine we got wasn't like the ones back in Phoenix at all. We had no designated area to do laundry, so again we chose positioning according to the weather. The only requirement was that it had to be near an electric outlet. We'd string the electric wire up to the outlet that was about five or six feet off the ground, fill the machine with buckets of water (hot and cold), put boiling soap in, let it swish around a few times (a few seconds to the left, then a few seconds to the right). Then, we'd drain the dirty water into the gutter that flowed out into the alley's gutter. Fill the machine again, *whish, whish* again. Drain again. Then wring by hand, and then hang. I know, it wasn't much different, but it is a few steps shorter anyway and every step counts in this situation.

On top of this process, before lifting the lid to the machine, we would carefully tap it with our fingertips. Tapping this way was the only safe way to check for any electrical current that might be flowing through it. I got zapped several times by the washing machine; most of the time it was only a tiny sting, but one time it shocked me so bad that my arm hurt for thirty minutes afterwards. Tapping was a necessary precaution.

Arrest Number One

I'd been in Pakistan for about a year and half, and although I was blissful about being away from David, I began having some strange issues with one of my brothers-in-law, Saad. Even now, I still don't understand what the *exact* issue was, but he honestly became unbearable. My language skills had developed a bit more by this time, so life around me was much more understandable and enjoyable—except for Saad. He started talking down at me and making ridiculous demands of me; I suppose it was just to see how far he could push me.

There's one particular time that stands out the most—it was the straw that broke the camel's back, as they say. Saad had come home after working in the field and headed straight for the cot in the courtyard. He laid back with great arrogance and propped his feet up with the soles of his feet pointing directly at me. (A huge insult in that part of the world.)

"Get me water," he demanded. Although I was used to doing things for all of the brothers in the family, I was a bit taken aback by his attitude. But I went and got the water and just ignored his way of asking.

"Get my cigarettes," he again barked out at me. Again, I did it.

But his attitude must've gotten on my last nerve that day, because it started a chain reaction. He started repeating this scene on a daily basis and making condescending remarks towards me. It was as if he wanted to provoke me. Gradually, I started rebelling against his condescending attitude, by telling him to do things himself. This only compounded the situation. He became more and more annoyed at my lack of compliance, causing our arguments to grow in intensity each passing day. Soon, I reached the end of my rope—something had to give. I decided that I wanted to go back home.

Going back to the States would be risky; after all, I was supposed to be under the radar—hiding with the kids. And I didn't know how Zain was going to take my decision of returning. By this time, our phone at home could make out-going calls to the States, so I called Zain and told him that I'd had enough.

"I miss my mom and everything in the States," I said. "I want to come home."

"Are you sure?" he asked me a couple of times to make sure I wasn't just being emotional.

"Yeah, absolutely! I can't take your brother anymore," I exclaimed.

He reluctantly accepted my decision and made the necessary arrangements for our return. I'll never forget that elated feeling—knowing I was going home. I couldn't wait to see my mom and hug her so tightly. Of course, I couldn't return empty-handed, so I went shopping and got some nice local gifts for everyone.

In hindsight, I realize that I'd let Zain's brother distract me from my true purpose of being there in the first place—a costly mistake that I'd soon regret.

Two or three weeks after the phone call, Zain picked us up at the airport in Phoenix. He took us to a tiny apartment that he'd rented somewhere in East Phoenix. I stayed at home each day because I knew that the authorities would be looking for us. The kids' pictures were posted on grocery stores bulletin boards and on the sides of milk cartons. My family related several stories about visits from police officers and FBI agents trying to locate us—along with their scare tactics and intimidating threats. But unbeknownst to me, they were already closing in—and fast. Apparently, the FBI had received a call informing them that I was back in Phoenix and that they were afraid I was about to run again. Within two weeks, it all came to a head.

***

The kids are playing in the living room—bouncing up and down again on the king size mattress on the floor. Zain is getting ready for work. A popular Hindi movie fills the air with music and ambiance. The kids are happily singing along and practicing their own versions of over-acting. Suddenly, the doorbell rings. Zain answers the door. It's a tall blonde woman; she seems pleasant enough.

"Hi. Is Thomas here?" she asks with a sweet smile. I look over Zain's shoulder to see her, out of curiosity, but I think nothing about it.

"No. No, Thomas lives here," Zain replies.

She glances over at me emotionless and says, "Oh, okay. Thanks." The door shuts.

The next morning about eight a.m., Zain leaves for work as usual. I'm taking the trash out to the back patio. The wall is six-feet tall, so I have no worries about anyone seeing me. I lean over to put the trash down on the ground and suddenly freeze when I hear a man's voice coming directly above my head.

"Marsha, open the door," a man says firmly.

I look up to the man, and my eyes fix on his badge. My heart sinks. I know I'm found. I go to the front door. There's a lump in my throat choking me. I open the front door and there she is—the same woman who was there the day before, but minus the sweet smile. She shows me her badge and says,

"Marsha, open the door. You're under arrest."

(I think they were FBI agents, but I honestly cannot remember what was on their badges.)

All I can think of at this point is about my children. "Please," I beg the woman, "you can't take them away. You don't understand!"

The man comes around to the front door, enters and sees me pleading with the woman. In attempt to calm me, the man says, "Don't worry. We just need to go down to the station and clear things up. The children will be back with you tonight. Now please put your hands together. We'll cuff you in the front and put something on top so we don't scare the children."

I can see the woman is over to the side of the room helping the kids put their shoes on. My legs are weak.

In a blink of an eye, I'm standing in a hallway at the police station. My hands are still cuffed and hidden under a sweater. I feel helpless. A man takes the two children firmly by the hand and begins walking them in the opposite direction of me. I am now in a mother's worst nightmare. All I can hear is my son's echoing cries to me, "Mommy! Mommy! Mommy! Mommy..." The cries get fainter with each step. The rest of my surroundings blur.

Next, I find myself standing in a holding cell with other women. Most of them are crying about their *own* children and trying to reach somebody on the phone to help. I find myself comforting others—telling them that everything will be okay.

***

I suppose I'm not surprised that they lied to me. They gave them back to David, and I didn't see my children again for the next three months. Again my poor choices hurt the ones I love the most.

Two Golden Bangles

It was 1993, and three intensive heart-wrenching months had gone by since my arrest. I still hadn't seen the children since then. The court hearings were confusing and excruciating. They made me look like a monster—one who'd taken her kids to some war-torn area of the world. They even blamed the trip to Pakistan for my daughter's front teeth falling out. (Hello?! She was five years old; they were *supposed* to come out.) And yet again, the biggest mistake I made was concealing the truth about David's history to the courts—disclosing the real reason I'd left Phoenix. I can still remember the judge looking right at me, telling me how wonderful a father he was. Inside I was burning alive, screaming for justice because I knew the *real* David. But sadly, I still couldn't face my deepest fears—I went along with the charade.

After accepting the plea bargain, I was given a year of probation and ordered to pay child support each month. Only then was I finally given permission to see my children again, but only through paid supervised visitation. The courts had deemed me a threat to my children's safety. These were difficult and disappointing times, indeed. I no longer knew anything about my children's daily lives. I shut out the world, constantly reliving the guilt of letting them down. I'd hit rock bottom and fell into a deep depression—creatively coming up with bazaar ways to end my life.

To help me cope with the guilt and loss, I threw myself into my work. I'd already started a job as a secretary for an insurance company, but decided to take on a second position with an answering service—to help pay for the supervised visits and child support. Being at home for even five minutes without Mona and Shedi was simply too painful bear. In a desperate attempt to soften the aching in my heart, I decorated two rooms for them—one in blue, and one in pink. I thought that somehow, they'd know that I was thinking about them—missing them—still loving them. But it didn't help. I'd sit lifeless, holding a stuffed animal and gazing in the distance—haunted by their laughter. Time was intangible.

After about five or six months, I was finally able to convince David that the money I was spending on visitation would be better spent on the kids themselves and not on some government agency. Thankfully, he agreed to let me meet with him in a public place instead, but according to his rules only. Nonetheless, I finally felt a ray of sunshine that I so desperately needed. I'd be able to spend more than an hour at a time with my children.

As fate would have it, David started dating one of the girls from my daytime job—the insurance company. They hit it off instantly, and at first, I was kind of glad. I thought she'd be a positive influence on him and that she might even convince him to let me have the kids back. But again, events took a wrong turn.

Things progressed quickly between them and they moved in together. And David did loosen up a bit—letting me take the kids home for one night on the weekends. That meant I could dote over them for a full twenty-four hours. I cherished each moment. But, that's when I started noticing the marks and bruises on their backs. When I questioned the kids what had happened, they explained that their new "mommy" had hit them with a wooden spoon. I was irate. But my hands were tied—in the court's eyes, *I* was the bad one.

I had to show proof, if anyone were ever to believe me. So, I started documenting my visits by taking pictures of the bruises. I began making calls to Child Protection Services to report what I knew, but my calls fell on deaf ears. I was frustrated, and my stress level began to run high. The kids would come home and relay uncomfortable stories of what was happening with their new family, events including David, my colleague and her children, particularly the older stepbrother. It was now a triple threat against my children. It was more than I could handle. In hindsight, I should've videotaped for the authorities what the kids were explaining to me. But I was a fool, and it just didn't occur to me at the time.

One day while dropping off the kids at David's, my former colleague came out of the home and confronted me. Her last comment that I remember was, "I'm tired of taking care of *your* kids." I fired back with full force. We began a screaming match right in the parking lot of their apartment complex. Before I knew it, I'd slapped her right across the face.

She began crying like a baby, screaming at the top of her lungs that she was going to call the police and have me arrested again. David ran out of the house to intervene and told me to leave so he could calm her down.

My endurance had reached its zenith. My continued phone calls to CPS had proven to be worthless.

The very next visit with my kids would change our lives forever. They described to me about having nightmares of being choked, and the continued beatings with a wooden spoon on their backs by their stepmother. I was heartbroken. How much more did they have to endure? Why wasn't CPS listening to me to my pleas?

That day, my children's plight broke me. I. I couldn't stand by any longer and wait for CPS to intervene. Documentation, pictures, and calls weren't ending their suffering. So, I decided to end it myself. I decided to go back—leave the country again. This time it would be for good. I wouldn't be so weak again. I would make it work, no matter what.

The next day, I set the wheels in motion. Luckily, I still had the passports from the last trip. The only problem was money for the tickets. All of my money had gone towards rent and child support. I had to think of something and fast. I looked at my arm and saw the golden bangle that

Zain had given to me as a gift. Actually, he had given me a set of two. I had one, and I had given the other to my mother. I went to my mother with a plan—and asked for her help.

"Mom, I can't take it anymore. I'm going back to Kalu," I explained, feeling heaviness in the bottom of my stomach.

"What? Again? Are you sure this is what you want to do, Sissie?"

"Yes, Mom. I have to."

"Alright. But you know that you will not be able to come back again. If you do, you'll go straight to jail. You know that, right?" I could hear the desperation in her voice.

"Yes. I know, Mom," I said with assurance. "I need some money for the tickets. I'm sorry to ask you for it, but, c-can I have the golden bangle back? I can sell it and use that money for the tickets."

Without any hesitation, my mother agreed, "Yes, of course. But I don't ever want you to go to jail for protecting those babies. You don't come back here for anything—not even for me. Do you understand?" She gently slid the golden circle from her wrist and reached out in surrender.

"Yes, Mom. I love you," I gently stammered out, realizing that there would be no turning back once I made this decision.

"I love you, Sissie. You take care of them babies," she said. I saw her pursing her lips together as though holding back her tears.

I sold the two golden bangles and booked the next available flight— for that coming Friday night—three tickets—Zain decided to stay. I packed what I could, just some of our clothes, three crocheted blankets that my mother had made for the kids, and my little blue dictionary. I was going alone so I had to pack light.

That Friday, we made our escape with perfect timing. My heart was pounding as the three of us boarded the plane and took our seats. The kids were ecstatic to hear they were going back to Pakistan, but I felt as if my heart would stop while we waiting for the plane to take flight. I was terrified that someone would be able to tell what I was doing—again. Tension and fear pierced me until the very second I felt the plane's wheels lift off the ground. Then, I knew we were on our way back to freedom.

(Amijon (far left), me (with the veil), Mom (middle) and Mona (driving the tonga). This picture was taken during my mom's first visit.)

Tough Love

I was blessed to have such an amazingly unselfish mother. She put me above her own needs every time—an astounding mother and best friend. But for one to have an amazing mother-in-law too is indeed a double blessing.

Only four feet tall (and probably four feet 'round, too) Amijon is a picture of survival. She was widowed in her 30's, with nine children, the youngest of whom never knew her father. Her hands were aged with years of physical labor, and her feet were thickly callused with cracks nearly half an inch deep—the result of being barefoot most of the time. She suffered from severe coughing spells and a weak heart—most likely from cooking over cow dung her entire life. She only wore traditionally modest clothing, and would only spend for herself what was essential—nothing more. Shampoo was deemed as an unnecessary luxury when the bar of laundry soap was readily available for her bath.

Her departed husband's children were her greatest dedication in life. I watched her cry many times for the ones that lived out of her home, and for the one that passed away.

"This belongs to my baby," she'd say as she held up an old yellowed baby shirt. Tears would swell up and trickle down her cheeks as she relayed the story of the baby who was sick with—as she described it—a mounting bump on his back. The baby died only a year into life.

I'm so proud to say that I learned so much from this humble and sickly woman. She taught me how to cook, clean, sew, fight, and shop—everything that I needed to know to survive.

Unfortunately, I didn't always understand Amijon. For the most part, during my first trip to Pakistan, I was treated like a real princess. Yet, after I arrived the second time, lots of things started slowly changing.

Upon my return to Kalu, I decided that if I were to stay this time, I'd have to have my own home separate from the rest of Zain's family. This was a must! The kids and I needed our own space where we could still have some independence in our lives. We needed our own traditions—our own ways of living. I called Zain in the States and explained how I felt, and asked for a separate home to be built. He agreed, and sent the money to start the construction.

We had to build our new home from the ground up. So, we bought the landfill area directly in front Amijon's front door. It took about ten months to build, but it felt like ten *years*; I don't really know for sure the exact amount of time it took to build—it's kind of a blur in my memory—all I know is that it took *way* too long. But we eventually moved into our new one-story two-room brick home, with a screened-in summer family room in the backyard. We loved it. I was able to be part of Zain's family but still have the privacy I needed. I had finally reached some real stability in life. The kids were in school again, we had our own home separate from the family, and Saad and I were on cordial terms again. Life was good.

Although we lived apart, we shared the same grocery bill with Amijon. Each day, I'd go eat with the family at her house and then take some food home for dinner as well. At my home, I'd only cook American cuisine whenever the urge struck me. I really had the best of both worlds. Until one day, out of the blue, everything changed.

***

"What are we cooking today?" I ask, gleefully bouncing into the courtyard, the same way I do every day.

"Well, *we* are cooking meat. And *you* are cooking meat," Amijon says.

I stop dead in my tracks and stand confused. "What do you mean?"

"Here's the meat and all the stuff that you need to go with it. Now, go home and cook it."

"Umm, wow. Okay." I'm shocked. It's been over a year since I've been back. This attitude is new and confusing. I stammer out, "I—I don't know how to cook."

"I'll tell you what to do." She runs through how to cook the meat. "First you…. Then you…. Then you….." This is all I hear without any understanding of what she's talking about. I reluctantly take the raw supplies back to my kitchen and attempt to make the stew from the memories of watching Amijon do it a thousand times over. I survive and manage to cook some concoction for dinner, but I'm still confused as to why I have to cook at my own home.

This scene played out several more times over the next couple of months. It was the first time in nearly two years I didn't feel one hundred percent welcome in mother-in-law's home. Thankfully, Amijon would come over every day to check on me—to see if I had any questions, or to help me with all of these new cooking techniques. Before I knew it, I was making my own bread, stew, rice, and sweets—everything on my own—whether I liked it or not.

Mona and Shedi were so patient and ate anything that I made, even though I was just learning. I knew it was not as good as their grandma's cooking, but they played along. Amijon kept teaching me—day after day.

It wasn't until about six months down the road that I finally had the courage to ask her why the change had occurred.

***

Amijon and I sit in the warm sun. Lunch is ready, and we're relaxing and having some tea. Amijon is lying on the *munja* with her shirt up exposing her stretch-marked stomach for fresh air—as is her habit when she is relaxing. I'm sitting on a small stool by her head. I'm looking intensely at her salt and pepper hair before I reach over and stroke her hair with my fingertips. It's coarse to the touch, most likely from years of washing it with laundry soap without any conditioner.

"Amijon. Why?"

"Why what?"

"Why did you separate me out from you like that? It seems like you don't love me anymore. But yet, I still feel that you love me. I'm so confused."

She rolls over onto her left side, putting her left arm under her head for support. She looks me in the eye and says, "Koltyni thee! (You are a donkey's daughter.)"

(It's much funnier in Hinkdo—trust me.)

"Look, Yasmine. I'm getting old, and Roni is going to be getting married soon. I don't know how long I'll be able to take care of you, and I know that no one else will. You're different from everyone around here, and others will always resent you because of it. Nobody will care if you go hungry or not. So, I'm teaching you how to take care of yourself, because one day I'll not be here to do it for you."

Both of us fall silent for a few seconds. I feel a knot in my throat as tears swell up. I finally speak up.

"Here I thought you were just being mean to me, but it was the exact opposite. Thank you."

That day, Amijon transformed from being my mother-in-law, to being just my *mother* through her love. She gave me so many wonderful things through my years with her, but the most important gift she gave me was survival.

I am who I am today because of the intercontinental fusion of two remarkable women, Mom and Amijon. I love them and miss them both very much.

(Amijon (left), me (middle), and Mom (right). This picture was taken
during my mom's first visit.)

Voodoo Chicken

Most people around the globe believe that some form of black magic exists. All cultures throughout history have stories and legends that passed down with each generation. Well, here's my story to pass down to my children.

***

It's springtime, 1990-something, and I'm at home doing laundry. I've just rinsed out one of my shirts and am hanging it on the wire to dry. I grip the bottom of the long shirt to straighten it out and feel something. *Hey, what is this?* It's a bump in the back flap corner. I pull it to me to get a closer look. *Hmm, this stitching is funny. And the thread is a different color, too. That's weird. It looks like it's been mended by someone. I've never had to fix this. Where did this come from?* The bump is hard and oddly shaped. It appears to have purposely been sown into my shirt.

I take the shirt over to Amijon's house to see if Roni knows anything about it. Roni is sitting outside in the sun. "Hey, Roni. What is this?" I ask sounding confused.

She grabs it and takes a closer look, flipping it over several times.

"I don't know." She then cries out to her mom, "Ami!" (Ami is short for Amijon). Amijon comes out of her room. "What is this?"

They inspect it together deeper. They're mumbling something to each other, but I can't understand them. Roni runs inside to her sewing machine and gets some scissors. She cuts open the corner of the hem, and pulls out an odd-shaped bone.

She blurts out, "A chicken bone!"

"What? A bone? How did that get in there?" I say.

Suddenly the speed of their conversation escalates, but the tone drops down to nearly a whisper. They're talking too fast for me to understand. Amijon grabs her veil and runs out the door with the bone and the shirt for someone who understands this kind of stuff better to examine it.

Roni calls me in closer and begins whispering to me. "It looks like black magic. Someone has purposely sewn in the chicken bone to put some type of spell on you."

"What? But who? Why?"

"We think we know who it was," says Roni, "but Ami is going to find out for sure. We think it is..." (Okay guys, wait. No need to mention names here. Anyway, we have no way to prove who it was. Anyone could have gotten my clothes off the line and sown a chicken bone so strategically in the back of my shirt. Right? So, on with the story.)

Amijon comes home about an hour later with great concern on her face. "We're going to the shaman tomorrow," she announces.

"What? Shaman? Where?" I ask, still in shock about all of this.

"He lives far away. It will take us two hours on a tonga."

We get up early the next morning; the tonga is already waiting for us. We veil up and head off to the shaman's village. Amijon has insisted that the two kids go with us too, just in case the hex is on them as well. They don't mind because they get to stay home from school and they love tonga rides.

The trip is long and hot. Two hours and a thousand bumps later, we finally arrive. The village doesn't look any different than the rest of the ones that I've seen before. But I'm a bit apprehensive as to what I'm about to experience. We stop in front of the shaman's home. It looks like a regular Pakistani home—with a courtyard, some trees and a few rose bushes—but the wall around the property is noticeably shorter than the rest. The shaman's wife greets us at the little white gate at the edge of the property. She's very polite and looks like the other local women. So far so good. She leads us to the main room. The room has a dirt floor and dishes are lined up against a shelf on the wall, as is tradition. There are two munjas, a couple chairs and a huge metal box for storage—again, nothing out of the ordinary. A welcoming touch of incense lingers in the room.

Over in the corner of the room, on the floor, there's a middle-aged man sitting on a rice mat. His salt and pepper beard is a bit rough, but neither too long nor too bushy. He's wearing a white long shirt with a collar and baggy drawstring pants, a typical Pakistani man's outfit, and a white prayer cap on his head. In his right hand, he's rotating some prayer beads, as do most religious folks in the region. The shaman doesn't stand up to greet us, but accepts a verbal greeting as we inch closer towards him. Out of respect, I only nod my head, saying nothing. We locate a place to sit on the mat directly in front of him.

Amijon begins to explain to him why we're here. She pulls up the knotted corner of her headscarf and unties it to expose the bone. "This is it," she says—the bone we found stitched into the corner of her clothes. She then dumps the bone onto his open palm.

Without any sense of surprise, he examines it closely, not saying a word: emotionless. To be perfectly honest, I'm waiting for him to break out with some chanting or dancing, but he doesn't. He sits quietly, staring at the dime-sized bone, flipping it around with his other index finger.

Suddenly, he gazes up us and says, "Yes, it's black magic. Probably a type of death spell. Whoever it is, is trying to make her sick enough to die. Chicken bones are often used for this type of spell."

My eyes pop open as big as silver dollars. I finally speak up. "What? Kill me? Why?"

"I'm getting the feeling that they are jealous of you." He stretches out his hand towards me and says, "Can I see your hands?"

I look at Amijon for approval. "Should I?"

"Yes. Let him look at them," she says.

I give him both of my hands very apprehensively and, quite frankly, skeptically. He looks deep into them with somber concentration. After about three minutes, he looks up at me and says, "You're running from something aren't you? Something in America."

A chill goes up my spine. *How does he know that?*

He continues, "You've had a lot of pain in your childhood."

All of sudden, time stops. I'm not in Pakistan anymore. My life flashes through my mind. The sexual abuse. The physical abuse. The mental abuse. I'm evidence of another generation scarred by domestic violence. Tears begin to well up in my eyes. I'm confused. Is he really seeing my life in my hand, or is this just karma messing with my mind?

I finally speak, "Yes, I have." I say this almost fearful that he just witnessed my inner visions along with me and now knows everything in my haunting past.

He tenderly and without judgment lets go of my hand and says with great confidence, "Don't worry. The spell is not going to kill you. This person who put the bone in your clothes cannot hurt you unless you let them. No one in life can hurt us unless we let them. We can take care of this spell today. You are going to live a very long life."

"Really?" I ask with almost belief in his gift. "How long will I live?"

"Your eighties," he replies with confidence and a smile. He then leans off to the side and grabs a pen and a small notebook. He writes several Urdu phrases in column formation along the edge of the paper. He instructs Amijon to put one of these phrases in bowl of water, and let sit for two hours. Then, we're to sprinkle the water around my home. If we do this routine for seven days, it should neutralize the spell that's been placed on me.

She thanks him intently, shaking his hand using both of her hands, while slipping him some money—just a few rupees as a gesture of appreciation. We quietly exit the room, and remount the tonga. I replay the event in my mind over and over. *How did he know that I was running from something? How did he know that I had a traumatic childhood?* I'm silent the entire ride home. My emotions are all over the place; worry, sadness, anger, embarrassment.

As soon as we reach home, Amijon fills Roni in on everything that occurred at the shaman's house. For the next week, Amijon handles all of the water directives for me.

Apparently, the cure worked—I'm still here. Thank God! Now let's see if I live to be at least 80.

(My bedroom.)

All I Want

Zain visited us in Pakistan from time to time over the years. The gaps between his visits were anywhere from five months to two years apart. For the majority of our marriage, he was simply a voice over the phone. (The only time that we really lived together for any *lengthy* amount of time, was in the States after my first arrest.)

The Internet finally made its way to my house in 2000, which brought about new problems for me. Zain had a tendency to hold a grudge against people very easily, and the Internet quickly became his catalyst for his short fuse. Whenever he'd need to vent about money or his family, he would call me on the computer. Even today, emails of his venting find my inbox. I hope that one day he can let go of such emotional discontent. But honestly, it was not always like that.

In fact, in the beginning of our marriage we were very much in love. When he came to visit us, he'd always ask if there was anything that we wanted from the States. Our requests were usually very funny stuff. You'd be amazed at what becomes precious after a few years in living in a farming community—on the other side of the planet.

Usually at the top of the list was cereal for the kids—Captain Crunch and Lucky Charms were especially popular. But with the cereal came the whining. As long as the cereal was in the house, the kids would drive me insane, wanting it every two hours. I was so thankful when that crap would finally run out—I couldn't stand their constant begging.

The second most popular items on our wish list were Twinkies and Ding Dongs. Believe it or not, I continued to ask for these up until 2013, just before I returned to the States. One day my boss in UAE did a run to Texas, and she was kind enough to ask me what I wanted. "Oh man, Ding Dongs and Twinkies! Nothing more!"

Next on our wish list was Kraft Macaroni and Cheese. Zain brought at least one huge suitcase full of it each time. Wow, what a treat that was!

Of course, food wasn't the only thing that we asked for. My two favorite gifts were a telescope and a waterbed mattress. The telescope actually became by best friend. On many lonely summer nights, I'd battle thousands of mosquitoes and gaze up at the stars for hours. I was an amateur astrologist, but I felt like Galileo—looking up at the endless black sparkling mass, plotting stars and catching glimpses of the planets whenever I could. I was able to see a couple of them quite vividly—like Venus, Mars, Jupiter and Saturn. I was also able to see the spot of Jupiter. *Amazing!* But Saturn is my personal all-time favorite. It literally took my breath away—she was tilted just enough to see her rings so clearly. A real heart-stopper! And of course, I would have to share all of my astronomical findings with the kids.

They weren't too interested in it, but they humored me nonetheless. We had some sweet family moments looking through the telescope together.

No doubt, the telescope was *my* preferred item, but amongst the *villagers*, the most popular was the waterbed Zain brought me. He couldn't bring a frame for it, so we built this really ridiculous looking one instead. It was so ugly, but didn't matter to me because it worked out just fine. We had no heater at all, so the water was stone cold in the wintertime. I'd have to put layers upon layers of bedding on top of it to keep us from freezing. The kids were in love with it too. They loved jumping on it, and would bring all the village kids over in small groups to get a glimpse of it. At one point, I think the bed had more visitors than I did. Even Amijon would bring family members over to my front door. She'd knock and say, "They want to see the waterbed." I guess I should've charged admission fees.

Unfortunately, some of the gifts that I received from America were just too painful to enjoy. Like a video tape that my mother had filmed for me that gave me a tour of all the decorative changes that she'd been making while remodeling her guest bathroom. I'll never forget the adorable peach colors. Yet, while normally anyone would love to sit and watch home movies of their mother, the heartache of missing my mother for me was simply too much. My heart broke in two whenever I watched anything from my homeland.

To survive, I tried to convince myself that I didn't care and that I didn't miss Arizona any more. I refused to watch anything from my family, or for that matter, *any* English programming on TV for several years. I found that my greatest defense was to simply reject the old and submerge in the new. Regrettably, I existed this way for many years. It wasn't until I moved to Dubai that I finally had the courage to gently crack my heart's closed door open just a hair and let that thin ray of yearning back in.

Godi Mommi

Children were everywhere in the village. Mostly they were family—Zain's nephews and nieces. There seemed to be hundreds of them. To this day, while chatting over the Internet, they still call me "Godi Mommi"—the white aunt.

True, they have the web now, but years ago in Kalu there were no Internet cafés or video games for kids to get lost in, and watching TV was frankly too dull. So, kids found good old-fashioned activities to blur the boredom away. Even for my children, the village was paradise. They were free to run around—knowing that there were always neighbors that looked out for them. They played all of the typical children's games like hide-and-seek, marbles, flying kites, and making mud-farts. The mud-fart game was my favorite activity to watch; it was hilarious, and was popular during the rainy seasons. The children would take an egg-sized ball of pliable mud, shaped it into a small bowl, spit in the center of it, and then slammed it on the ground upside down. If done correctly, the air pocket would burst out the top with a loud farting sound—and there you have your mud-farts. Always good for a laugh.

Anyway, you remember I explained earlier that I built my home separately from the family, right? Well, the whole point of that was so I could practice some of my own culture—being able to provide a balance for the kids. We'd already taken on all of the traits of Zain's family. We walked like them and talked like them; but I still wanted to remain rooted in some American practices. One of the many American customs that I took with us was the beloved tooth fairy tradition. When my kids lost a baby tooth, I'd put money in place of that sweet little treasure. A simple concept? Right. Yes—it usually is—until the neighborhood kids find out that you're giving money away for children's teeth. (Oh, yes. You know where this is heading.) We all know that kids do crazy things. They watch others, and then copy what they see. Sometimes this can be a good thing. And, well, here's an example when it wasn't and things went horribly wrong.

***

I hear some small tapping on the metal screen doorframe and open the door to find a little boy about eight years old standing there. "Yes?" I said.

"Godi mommi, look!" he says with great exuberance as he shoots his hand up high for me to see. He is holding a tooth with a bloody end. He squeals again, "I have a tooth. Can I have some money for it?"

"What?" I say, confused. It hasn't dawned on me where he would have gotten this idea. Suddenly, it comes to me. I gasp. *Oh no! What has Shedi done now?*

My son had lost his tooth the day before and—being a good mother, holding true to tradition—I told him that the tooth fairy would come and get it. That night, the tooth fairy came (*wink wink*), and she put the money under his pillow for him to find. The next morning, he ran outside and told all of his friends that *I* gave him the money for his tooth—totally leaving out the whole tooth fairy bit. Apparently, the word got around really fast that I was giving out money for children's teeth. The next two hours were total chaos. Kids all over the neighborhood went wild, instantly creating ways to pull out each other's teeth. When their families questioned them about what they were doing, the kids answered, "Godi mommi wants them."

Not long after, irate women flooded my mother-in-law's home, bellowing at the top of their lungs—and understandably so. Arms and veils were flapping everywhere. All hell had broken loose in Kalu that morning. Amijon had to calm all of them down and try to explain to them that I was innocent and just upholding my own cultural traditions. What a nightmare that was!

All soon forgave me, and the village kids continued to be an important part of my life. When Mona and Shedi were about ten and eleven, I was a bit disappointed that the kids didn't have any Brownie or Boy Scout Troop in the area. So, I decided to launch my own version of Brownie Troop for the village girls. I bought massive amounts of brown material for uniforms and passed it out to all of the girls in the village who wanted to take part in the group. Each girl had her own uniform sewn-up at home. We had group meetings in my home once a week. We'd sing, play games and eat snacks. We even had our own theme song that my daughter Mona had written. "*Hum brownie group hai* (we are the brownie group)" that we'd sing at the top of our lungs. It was a hit! But the boys of the neighborhood felt a bit left out and I knew it.

Soon, I opened a learning center right in my own backyard for *all* of the neighborhood kids. We had a library, fish tank, English classes, and played sports. I can't tell you how amazing and fulfilling it was. Surprisingly, my favorite thing to do was to teach the kids how to play baseball. We set up the four bases in the back yard and played for hours. *Good times indeed.*

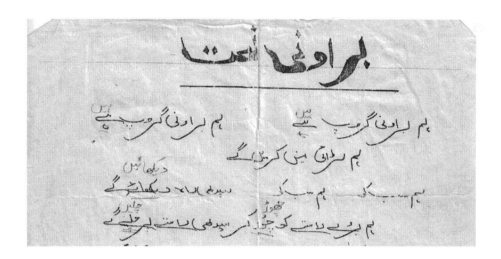

(The Brownie Group theme song, written by Mona. Found this original
photocopy in my files.)

(The kids ready for school.)

Welfare Check

It was 1990-something in Kalu around seven o'clock in the morning when a man and a woman from the American State Department unexpectedly came to our village to check on the kids' welfare. They claimed they'd found my home by asking someone in the nearest big city. I could just imagine the conversation that took place.

"Hey, do you know this white lady?" they ask some disheveled man on a donkey, probably showing him my mugshot.

"Oh, Gori Yasmine?" the farmer says as he pets his obedient animal. "Yeah, everyone knows her. Just follow that road. Turn left. Then right. Keep bumping down

the dirt road. You can't miss it. It's the big red three-story house in the middle of all the ancient ruins."

Alright. Maybe that's not *exactly* how it happened, but they found me nonetheless. We'd already moved into our new home across the way by this time, and the kids were getting ready for school. If I remember correctly, I was pumping water from the hand pump in my kitchen, when I heard my brother-in-law, Rafi, knocking on my metal door.

"*Bobbi,* [*bobbi* meaning sister-in-law]" he says. "There are some white people here to see you." He has an anxious look on his face.

"What?! Who?!" I blurt out in shock. A wave of electricity rages through my body. "Oh my God, they've found me," I mumble under my breath.

"I don't know who they are," he continues. "They want to see you, Mona, and Shedi. Come. They want to see you right now." He turns and walks away. My legs lose all power.

My mind races, searching for what I should do next. My body radiates tremors, like thousands of little aftershocks after an earthquake. Suddenly, I have an idea. *I'll nail the windows shut so they can't get in and grab the kids.* I run to the toolbox and snatch the hammer and nails. *Bang! Bang! Bang!* I desperately nail the kitchen window shut. The kids are standing in the hallway, just looking at me in daze. By this point, I am totally delirious.

"Don't let anyone in this house!" I scream at them. "Do you understand?" The kids nod in agreement. "Even if a white person comes to the door, don't open it! Okay? Only for me! You can *only* open the door for me."

I open the alleyway door, step outside and have them lock it. My tremors continue, making it difficult for me to walk. I know that there's no extradition treaty between the United States and Pakistan, but I'm still so terrified. I go to Amijon's courtyard, where they're waiting for me. As I walk towards them, I think, *What if they take me? What if they try to take the kids? Should I run?*

I first extend my hand to the male visitor; he shakes it firmly. He's dressed in business attire and looks like he is in his 30s and physically fit. I then move over to the woman—who is also wearing business clothing, but with a skirt—and she too shakes my hand firmly. She's bit older—appearing in her early 40s. Standing a bit off to the side is a middle-aged Pakistani gentleman, serving as a Hindko translator from the American Embassy in Islamabad. I look over at him—and while keeping true to local customs—I simply nod my head in greeting. He returns the gesture.

The woman starts. "Marsha, we're from the State Department. We're here to see the children."

I blurt out, almost interrupting her, "But you can't take them. There's no extradition treaty here."

"That's correct," she says. "But we're not here to take them back to the States. We're only doing a welfare check to see the condition of the children and report back to the State Department and their father. We just want to see them and make sure that they are okay—eating well and going to school."

A bit taken aback and very apprehensive, I say, "Of course my children are going to school. We're happy here."

"Can we see them?"

"I don't know. I'm afraid that you'll try to take them. I don't trust anyone anymore."

The man intercedes and tries to assure me, "No, we can't do that. We are only here to do a welfare check and report it to their father. That's it."

I feel a burning pit in my stomach. Where in the hell were these people when I needed them in Phoenix? Now we're finally happy, and now they want to check the welfare of my children?

I look at Rafi as if to ask what I should do. He nods in assurance that everything will be fine. I take the small group of visitors over to my home to meet with the kids. I knock on the door and assure them that it's okay to let me in. They meet the children and chitchat a bit, take a tour around the house, and that's it. The visit is over and the uninvited guests leave without drama.

They did as they first explained; they were only there to check the wellbeing of the kids. I never received a copy of their report, but this was only the first of several spot-checks that they would do. The kids even started calling the translator from the embassy "Uncle" because he was in touch with us so often. The embassy kept tabs on me from that point on, but the actual welfare checks stopped when the kids were in their teens. I had confirmation that David knew where we were located from that point on, but we never heard from him directly. No phone call. No mail. No money. Nothing. If he did send anything, it never reached *us*.

(Me and my mommy during her first visit.)

The Lie

My mother was an amazingly brave lady. She suffered a disturbingly abusive childhood, but was able to overcome it all and become the greatest mother of all time. I love her so much.

She came to visit me twice in Pakistan during my fourteen years in the village. The first time was in 1998. She came with Zain on one of his trips home. We'd just moved into our *second* new home—a farmhouse in the countryside, about a forty-five minute walk from the small village home.

(This farmhouse had always been Zain's dream—to build a large enough home for the entire family for all five brothers, their wives and children.)

I was ecstatic to see my mom again. I couldn't wait to show her all of the exotic things about my new life. But it wasn't as pleasant for her as I'd envisioned. My mother had an extremely difficult time adjusting. Between the weather and the culture shock, she was in total disarray.

It was the dead of winter, and we had no electricity in our country home. We used lanterns at night and built fires to stay warm—quite primitive actually. Now that I think about it, I was a real idiot to think that my mother would be comfortable there. I think we can mark this one up as another stupid decision on my part.

The biggest downfall of the whole scenario at farmhouse was that it had no American-style toilet—as if no electricity and no heat were not bad enough. Out of desperation to solve the toilet issue for her, we took an old wooden chair with a wicker woven-type of seat and cut a hole through the middle. This was so she could sit on it and *go* into a silver pan below—something like a deep-dish pizza pan.

(Mona practicing taking out the trash.)

Like I was saying, my mom was having a really hard time with her first visit. On the second day, she wanted to go home; I honestly couldn't blame her. I messed up. She was freezing to death and running a fever. We decided to move her to my sister-in-law's home in the village and put a heater in her room. Then, as she wished, we moved her plane ticket up a week so she could go home early. To do this, Zain had to take her passport along with her original ticket to the travel agent.

My mother was not only suffering physically, but she was starting to break down emotionally as well.

"Where's my passport?" She asked me almost angrily.

"I had to give it to the travel agent to change your ticket. Remember?"

"I want to talk to the American Embassy. Right now."

"What? Why?"

"Because, you're holding my passport from me."

"What? No, I'm not! I just told you that I had to give it to the agent to change your ticket."

"So why don't I have it yet?"

"I don't know. It takes a few days here."

"I want to see it right now. I think you're holding me here against my will."

"What? No! Mom! You wanted to leave early, right? So the man needs the passport to change the ticket."

By the third day, my mom was *really, really* losing her patience. Things were getting tenser by the hour. She wasn't feeling well as it was, she thought I was holding her captive, and people were making matters worse by coming in to watch her sleep. The entire ordeal was freaking her out. I needed to get my mother on the next plane—for sure. Zain had finally gotten her ticket booked for the upcoming Friday at one p.m. So we thought.

***

It's Friday morning, about seven a.m. It's still bitter cold outside, but my mom has a renewed spring in her step this morning as she packs her stuff to go home. The car will be here at nine a.m. to take us to the airport. I step outside to get some morning air. My husband walks into the courtyard.

"I have some bad news," he says in a sober voice—almost apologetic.

"What?" I can tell something is wrong.

"Your mom has missed her plane."

"What?" I'm even annoyed at the thought of him trying to be funny at a time like this. "No. It's nowhere near one p.m. We have plenty of time to get there."

"No, her plane left last night."

"What?! How? What do you mean?"

"I read the ticket wrong. I thought it said one p.m. But, it says one a.m."

"Are you serious!? What am I going to tell my mother? She already thinks I'm holding her here against her will." I'm shocked. I hold my hand up with the palm facing Zain.

"I need to think for a minute."

I pace back and forth, while mumbling to myself. Suddenly, I have an idea. I walk to my mom's room and open the door. I'm heartbroken and scared; she's still packing and looking brighter than I've seen her since her arrival.

"Mom," I say softly.

"Yeah, Sissie," she says, without looking up.

I enter slowly and choose my words carefully. "You know that we're in Pakistan, right?"

"Yeah."

"And you know that almost anything can happen here, without any notice or anything; and without any explanation at all."

"Yeah, I know," she says, still arranging her baggage.

"Well, something's happened," I say as calmly as I possibly can, knowing that all Hell is about to break loose.

My mom looks up. "What? What's wrong?" She looks terrified.

"Benazir Bhutto has closed all airports—all of the flights have been cancelled. No one can get in *or out* of Pakistan." I try to speak as confidently as possible, hoping that she will buy my story. I figure that if I blame it on the government, she's more likely to accept it.

"What?! They can't do that?!" she yells, almost as if she's asking me. It seems like she's going to cry.

Sensing that she's accepting this absurd lie, I start flapping my arms about. "Yeah, Mom. It's crazy, I know. But all the airports are closed across the country. You know, presidents can do that here. Don't worry. Zain is going to get you another ticket booked for you as soon as possible. He's going to the ticket office right now to see what is going on."

My mom sits on the side of the bed. All of the strength has left her legs. I walk over to her, put my arms around her, and squeeze.

"I'm sorry Mom."

But inside, I was actually saying: *I'm sorry Mom for letting you down again.*

I never told my mom the truth about that day. Instead, I spent the rest of my mom's visit closely with her—feeling guilty and trying to keep her assured that she didn't need to talk to the embassy. We managed to get her booked on the next flight out. I was heartbroken to see her go, but knew it was for the best. She finally made it home safe and sound.

300 Falling Stars

Over the span of those fourteen years abroad, we dealt with a lot of natural elements like rain, hail, some snow, and lunar and solar eclipses. Of course, for most of us, these are exciting and understood. But for people like Amijon, it's a completely different story. For instance, during a solar eclipse, Amijon was worried that the world was ending. She was old-fashioned that way and just didn't accept scientific explanations for these types of things; it was part of her charm.

(Amijon in the courtyard.)

During my stint with astrology, around December in 2000, I'd read online that there was going to be a meteor shower in our part of the hemisphere. I was overjoyed and couldn't wait to see it. I had two days to plan it all out. The kids and I would lie on the roof of the third story and watch the shower as a family. I'd also have all of the blankets and stuff prepared ahead of time to make sure we were warm and cozy; after all, it was December.

Sometime the next night, I woke up to get some water from the kitchen and looked outside the window to gaze upward. Just then, at that very moment, I saw a falling star. *Hmmm. That's sweet. What are the chances of seeing a shooting star the very moment I am looking out the window?* But then suddenly it came to me that the meteor shower was supposed to be happening the very next night. *Wait, or is it tonight?* I began to think that I might have messed up on my calculations. I waited a few more moments and continued to stare upward. About five minutes later, I saw another falling star. *Okay, that did it*

"Get up! Get up! The meteor shower is happening tonight, right now!" I screamed throughout the house.

It was two a.m., but I didn't care. I woke the two kids up, scrambled to get the blankets together, and started toting the gang up the three flights of stairs. The kids were around nine and eleven years old at the time, so they weren't that excited when I woke them up, especially since they had to help carry blankets up the stairs, too— Zain wasn't there to help. Nevertheless, I didn't want them to miss the show.

Climbing slowly, we finally reached the roof and bedded down. The meteor show was incredible. As a group, we began counting the falling stars. Three hundred and thirty, in fact. Some of them were larger than life—appearing to be coming right for us. *Ssshhhhhew!* The sound was kind of unnerving as they zoomed over our heads and into the blackness. They felt so close. What a spectacular show! We were amazed and in awe. I had never seen such an event before, or since. We hung there watching, counting, and chatting until dawn—when the stars were too light to see any longer. Three and a half beautiful hours never to be forgotten.

In contrast, the scariest natural element that we dealt with was the tornado of 2002.

We were asleep in our beds in the downstairs living area. It was around one a.m. when the thunderstorm woke me up. It sounded like a pretty severe storm, but I wasn't scared at all. I knew we were safe on the first floor. I could hear the wind outside getting stronger and stronger—and louder and louder. The kids woke up and quietly sat up in bed just looking at me for assurance.

"It's alright. Don't worry," I said. "It'll pass in a few minutes." But I was wrong.

The noise outside quickly escalated; turning into a roar that sounded like a train coming over the house. By this time, I was getting a bit nervous myself. The living room's French doors were jarring violently back and forth. Suddenly, the latch unhooked and the doors exploded open as if someone had kicked them in.

"Oh my God!" I screamed.

I jumped out of bed and ran over to grab the doors and pull them shut with all of my might. The wind was so strong, but I finally got them closed and latched. All of us were so scared. We all started praying.

We heard violent crashes outside. The French doors continued to jerk—as if possessed by demons. The doors exploded open a second time—breaking the lock clean off. Again, I jumped up, and with desperation, I pulled the couch in front of the doors to hold them closed. I didn't know what else to do. I was terrified, praying that the couch would hold. By this time, the kids had united on one bed. I joined them and we huddled together, cowering in murmurs, calling on God. Then as quickly as the storm came, the roar ended. It was silent again.

The next morning, everyone viewed the damage throughout the village. Walls around the neighborhood fell down; the cement slab on our upstairs water tank flew off and ended up in some neighbor's yard. Sadly, one woman was said to have died in the tornado. She'd gone on her roof to save her cow dung patties from getting wet. They never found her.

Heart Attack

My mother was forgiving and courageous enough to visit me in Kalu once again in 2001. This time she was coming for Roni's wedding. It had been a couple of years since her last visit. By this time, we'd moved back to the smaller home in the village because we weren't able to get the electricity properly hooked up at the farmhouse. Of course, not wanting to repeat the pains of the last time she visited, I made sure that the home was stocked and ready to go—it was going to be perfect. And it was. Until...

It's eleven p.m., and my mother calls out to me from the other room, "Sissie. Come here."

"Yes, Mom."

"I'm—I'm having pains in my chest." Her voice is soft and stammering. "I think I am having a heart attack." I'm confused because she had seemed just fine earlier, but her eyes are telling me differently now. Her pain intensifies. "I—I think I should get to the hospital."

I rush for help.

Zain calls for a car, which arrives in fifteen minutes. (No ambulance service is available in the area.) I help my mother into the backseat. I join her from the opposite side. Zain sits up in the front with the driver. We head to the nearest doctor's home which is in the very next town—only minutes away.

My mom hunches to one side with her hands pressed against her chest as she tries to breathe through the pain. I put my arm around her for support.

"We're almost there, Mom," I try to console her. I'm frustrated that I cannot do any more at this point.

We pull up outside the doctor's home. The house is blackened and quiet. The driver knocks on the front door and rings the bell twice. No one answers. The driver tries again. Finally, I can see a man open the door. He speaks to the driver for a minute and shuts the door. The driver turns around and returns to the car to explain.

"The doctor refuses to open the door to us. He says that he doesn't see patients at this time of night."

"What!" I scream out. "How do you turn patients away? And one that's having a heart attack, no less! Is he serious? Can he do that?"

Zain turns to me and says, "Our only alternative is to take Sandi to the Air Force Base hospital, but it's about thirty minutes away."

My mother shakes her head in agreement. Zain instructs the driver and we go as quickly as possible to the next hospital. I hold my mother in my arms, wishing I'd never asked her to come back to visit me. My mother is not speaking a word. The only thing I hear is a moan now and then. I can't hold back any longer—tears begin streaming down my face. All I want is for her to be okay.

Painfully we go through the required checkpoint. We arrive at the hospital's emergency area, and we help her in. They take her, hook her up to some machines, and give her some kind of medicine. I am a basket case, talking to myself in the waiting room. *This is all my fault. Why did I let her come again?*

The doctor comes out, "It's a mild heart attack, and she needs to stay the rest of the night."

I look to Zain and say, "I'll stay with my Mom. You can go and come back in the morning." He leaves.

My mother lies in the bed, machines monitoring her every beat and breath. The smell of iodine lingers in the air around us. She's resting peacefully with her eyes closed as I reach over and caress her head. Her gray, curly hair is soft to touch, and the locks effortlessly bounce back into place. She's pale, but she's okay. I know deep down that she has to leave Pakistan—has to leave *me*—again. I feel that this is most likely the last time I'll see my mother alive. I know that she'll not be strong enough for one more visit; I won't even let her try. I touch her hand and memorize the bluish bulging veins and the shape of her long piano fingers and yellowish nails. Hers is the first hand that ever showed me love in this world, and I'm helpless in returning such dedication to her.

There are no chairs on which to sit, so I quietly remove the *chadur* from my head and lay it on the floor. I lie down on the sheet, using my curled-up arm as a pillow, and breathe a sigh of heavy guilt. The cement floor is cool and hard. I drift off to sleep

(Me and my mommy during her second visit—the day before her heart attack. This was our last photo together.)

The next morning, I told my mother that she had to go back to the States, because I couldn't risk anything else happening to her. She didn't try to argue; she too knew it was for the best. We arranged her ticket, and she made the next available flight.

At the departure gate, we held each other tight not wanting to let go. I could barely breathe—the lump in my throat was overpowering. Tears were streaming down. My world was crashing down around me. Heartbroken and without saying it aloud, we both knew it would be our last time on this Earth together. (It was.)

"I love you Sissie."

"I love you mom."

(Left photo: Nudul with Amijon. Right photo:
Shedi, me, Nudul, and Mona.)

Say What?

In 2002, the greatest surprise of all happened to our family—my son, Nudul, was born. It was incredible having a baby around the house after all of those years. He was like a refreshing brook that flowed through our home, bringing in new life and spring aromas. He was a tiny baby; and many doubted that he would survive. I doted over him as if he was my first child. Zain came home for Nudul's circumcision, but quickly left us again as usual.

About a year later, Shedi, now sixteen, came to me with a certain request.

"Mom, I want to go to America. Everyone keeps asking me why I'm here. I'm sick of it! Why am I here? I want to go live in America where I belong."

I guess I knew down deep there would come a time when he'd make such a request. Although my heart screamed out for him not to leave, I agreed to let him go. After all, he was not my prisoner. He was a young man now, and I could see that this was what he really wanted to do. But we had a lot of preparations to do first.

All three of our passports and visas had expired about eight years prior, so the first thing on our list was to get his passport renewed. We called the American Embassy and got an emergency travel passport issued for him. Within two weeks of his request, my son fulfilled his dream of going back to America. He went and lived with his father. As for what happened there, only my son can tell his story. But as for me back in Pakistan, I cried every single day. I felt as if all of my breath had left my body.

That life-changing event inadvertently started a chain reaction within my own life. Shedi's absence made me realize how much I had grown dependent on *him* and the *other male members* of the family. I, like a fool, had passively surrendered my independence in life, and hadn't even recognized it. I'd been provided with everything I needed—food, shoes, clothing, medicine, etc. I'd been told whom I could have for friends and whom I couldn't. I'd absorbed my surroundings so much that I'd literally melted in the background. I looked like the villagers. I talked like the villagers. And I had finally learned how to walk like the villagers. Which is not bad in *itself*—but I'd forgotten who *I* was in the process. I was not Marsha anymore. I'd succumbed to the very thing my mother had warned me years earlier. I had no self-identity. No passport. No visa. No husband.

I should explain here, that losing my self-identity did not happen suddenly; it happened over the fourteen years—very gradually. Maybe I just gave up hope of ever returning to my homeland, or maybe I was just too comfortable; I don't know. I guess I'll never *really* know why I let it happen.

So, there I was in 2002—sitting alone in Kalu with my one-year-old son and a teenage daughter. Shedi was gone. My so-called marriage to

Zain was basically non-existent and he'd even started showing violent tendencies on his last few visits. (One day while I was protecting Shedi from him, he'd dragged me by the hair and threw me out in the alley—for all of his family to see. He'd started to change and I didn't understand why.) To make matters worse, I'd recently received some news informing me that he was going to marry a second wife—the *good friend* that he'd been talking about lately. I was confused—and hurt, but not surprised.

There was one afternoon I'll never forget when I glanced up to the top of my house's garden wall and realized that its coiled barbed wire was mocking me. *Yasmine, you're not free; you've actually created your own prison. No one can get in. And you can't get out.*

It all came to a head the day I was cooking lunch and realized that I'd run out of tomatoes. For whatever reason that particular day, I stepped out of my boundaries and went to the shopping myself. I simply didn't *want* to wait for the *men* to do it for me. I hailed a *tonga* and went to my brother-in-law's vegetable store in Hazro. I got what I needed and headed back home. It took only an hour. *No big deal, right?* For the first time in years, I had gone somewhere alone—the kiss of independence softly kissed me on my cheek and whispered, *"I've missed you."*

My pride was soon squashed as soon as the brother-in-law, Uzaif, got home. He began scolding me for my having gone to the store and getting tomatoes.

"You've embarrassed this family!" he yelled.

That was basically the last sentence I heard. Just like Charlie Brown's teacher, his voice had turned into incomprehensible murmurs. My eyes had glassed over. Suddenly I realized that I had been in the village for fourteen years. My thoughts overcame me. *Where did all of that time go? What have I done with my life? Who am I? I really did lose my identity. Wait, what am I still doing in this village? I've got to get the kids and me out of here.*

As soon as Uzaif left the house, I jumped on the phone with Zain and told him that I wanted out of the village immediately. I wanted to move to the capitol Islamabad—about an hour and a half away—where most of the other Westerners lived. Not just that I *wanted* to go, but I *had* to go. I'd die if I didn't!

Surprisingly, the voice on the phone agreed quite easily. He then instructed his family to take me to Islamabad and find a place for me to live. Of course, the family tried their best to convince me to stay; they told me all kinds of scary stories. But I wouldn't listen; I'd had enough and needed a change. I had to move—with or without their blessing. So I moved.

I took a penthouse apartment in the Westerner's section of the city. It was amazing! Luxurious marble floors and chandeliers—what a change from Kalu! In a snap, I'd gone from living in humble village surroundings, straight into the life of the elite posh. When I bought eggs, it wasn't just one or two eggs anymore; it was one- or two-dozen. *Woohoo!* I'd finally made it to the big time. Zain could do whatever he wanted with his new fiancée now. I really didn't care anymore. I'd started my new life.

Beverly Hillbillies

I felt like a cat with nine lives. Again, I'd found a new life in a new exciting city—and to top it off—I was driving again! True, the round a bouts made me dizzy, and it took me a while to get used to driving on the left side of the road, but I caught on eventually. It was awesome! I'd traded in the dirt floors of Kalu for the white marble floors of the upper side of the Islamabad. The days of Amijon banging on my front door with a brick to wake me up, were gone. Instead, I had a private elevator that went directly to my door and a chime doorbell. *Classy!*

Now, we were settled in—just my daughter, my youngest son, and me. We lived directly across from a strip mall. It was exciting to see some of the old brand names from my own homeland. Dunkin' Donuts—a view away! How amazing was that?

Zain's new marriage plans had finally made me realize that he was unpredictable and that it was time for me to start supporting myself financially. I didn't know if he was ever coming back to Pakistan or not, but I was 100% sure that our marriage was over. It was simply a legal issue at this point. It'd already been almost three years since his last visit to see Nudul.

My first step to financial freedom was to get a job. Thankfully, a new Islamabad friend helped me look for one. I met him in Dunkin' Donuts after spying over his shoulder while he was working on his shiny new laptop. Keep in mind; I'd never seen one before.

I remember asking him, "Hey, is that a com-pu-ter?"

He turned his head towards me and gave a long, strange look as if I had just gotten off the boat or something—which was kind of true, in a way. Anyway, a couple of weeks later after I mentioned to him that I was looking for a job, he offered to take me to one of the biggest call centers in town—Touchstone Communications. He explained to me that they made calls to the United States and that they needed American accent trainers.

"Oh, wow! That's great. I can do that," I said. "Let's go."

With my youngest son in tow, we went down to Touchstone's office and I applied for a training position with confidence; I got the job immediately. I started that week teaching American accent classes to customer service representatives. We all worked the graveyard shift, which turned out to be great fun. But I can honestly say, it was challenging being a single mom working the graveyard shift. My typical day was like this—I worked all night, came home, got the kids off to school, slept for four hours, got back up, and then brought them back home. Like I said, doing this daily routine, and surviving on only four hours sleep, was challenging; but I worked it like a pro.

(At my desk inside Touchstone Communications. 2005.)

I really enjoyed my new job, and took a liking to training as well. It was a great career rebirth for me. The office was modern, with amazing glass walls and doors throughout. Once again, I felt a new sense of freedom and independence in Islamabad; and now I had importance, too.

At first, I was driving a beat-up old red mini-van we called the *carry-dubba* that I'd brought with me from the village. It was the working van for the farmhouse; but it was now mine. It was extremely trying on my patience, and humiliating to say the least. It kept overheating, and I had to stop and lift the driver's seat up to work on the engine. Luckily, I was finally able to talk Zain into sending me some cash so I could get a decent car that was more user-friendly. I bought a brand-new Suzuki Mehran. It was a lovely shade of blue that matched my eyes—and more importantly—no more breakdowns! I loved that car.

Both of the kids were in the same school together—Mona was in high school and the Nudul in kindergarten. This unusual grade-combination made me pretty popular amongst the staff. Overall, life was going really well. Islamabad was growing nicely on us. But then there was a surprising phone call from Shedi.

"Mom, I wanna come home," he said.

"What?" I said in total disbelief and utter confusion. "I thought you wanted to go to America?"

"Things aren't working out like I thought they would," he stressed. "I wanna come home!"

Without any hesitation, I said, "Okay, son. I'll get your plane ticket today. See you soon."

The Truce

Shedi arrived back in Pakistan safe and sound, and the first thing he needed was a set of wheels. He didn't have a driver's license, but to be honest, neither did a lot of people. Besides, we were from the boonies and he'd been driving around the village for years. So, against my better judgment, I bought him a brand new motorcycle. He was elated, but I still chalk this decision up as another one of my biggest mistakes.

Just as I felt a new sense of freedom in Islamabad, so did my son, Shedi. During his trip to the States, he'd suffered from culture shock; just like anyone else would have. He was glad to be back where he felt more at home; after all, he'd grown up in this part of the world. But unfortunately, he started running around with the wrong crowds. I was really worried about him but had little control over what he did, and whom he did it with. *Teenagers!* He soon took a job at one of the other call centers in town—working the graveyard shift like me. He'd only worked there two days when our life took another turn down a very wrong road. It happened like this.

***

It's about ten p.m., and Shedi is riding his new motorcycle to work, when he doesn't yield to a yellow light, and just goes through it. He quickly gets pulled over by two local police officers. One thing leads to another, and a heated argument begins between Shedi and one of the officers. Shedi lacks respect for authority, and unfortunately, he's met a dark rival tonight. The officer raises his hand to strike him. Instantly in defense, Shedi blurts out a string of obscenities.

"That's it! You're under arrest!"

"You can't arrest me. I'm an American,"

"No, you're not! If so, then how do you speak Urdu so well?"

"I was raised in Pakistan!"

"You're lying!"

"No, I'm not. I'm calling my mother and you'll see." He dials my number. "Mom, they're arresting me! You have to come down here right now!" he screams.

He gives me his location, and with lightning speed, I grab my veiling and the other two kids. Together we race to the intersection about three miles away. I can see the small crowd of men. I jump out of the car and run to where they are still arguing. All I can think is, *I have to get my son away from the police.*

I run up to the officer and begin begging him in Hindko to release my son. "Please! Please! You have to let him go with me!"

"No I don't. He was rude to me. I'm taking him in to the jail," he says as he angrily jerks to the right, pointing at the paddy wagon that my son is being pushed into. Shedi looks back at me with fear in his eyes.

"Mom. Tell him I'm from America!"

The officer screams back at him, "You are Afghani! And I know it!"

I continue to beg. "No. We are American. Why won't you listen to me? Please! Say whatever you want! However much money you want, but do not take him!"

"I'm not letting him go. We're going to teach him a lesson. He's coming with us."

My pleas have failed. I'm not helping my son. They're taking him anyway. The officer won't believe that I'm American—*my* language skills are too good as well. With our light-colored skin and blue eyes, they think we're from Afghanistan, not America. They close the door of the paddy wagon. I'm desperate and don't know what to do. There's no way that I can follow them to the police station straightaway—I can't risk taking my daughter there. I have to make the decision to take her home first.

I speed home, knowing that every second counts if I'm going to save Shedi. I grab our passports out of the drawer and run downstairs to get a male neighbor to go with me—even I can't risk going alone. Suddenly, my cell phone rings again.

I answer in a snap. "Hello!"

"Mom," I hear in a deep, sober voice. "You have to come now. They're beating me, Mom. Bring my passport. They don't believe that I'm American. They think that I am Pathan."

The line goes dead. I'm horrified. The man downstairs and I rush to the car, and we go as fast as we can.

We arrive at the station and run towards the building. I burst through the double doors. "I demand to see my son right now. Where is he? Where is my son?"

I produce our passports to prove who we are. The officer's face changes color right on the spot. He realizes that they've just made a huge mistake.

He tries to weasel through the situation. "Well, madam, you see, he was rude to the officer, and we tried to calm him down. That's why we took him in."

"I want to see my son right this minute," I demand again. The officer makes a call and instructs them to bring in my son. I can hear him mutter into the receiver, "*Woh Amreecan hai.* (He is American.)"

The door to the right of me opens, and I jerk my head over to see if it's Shedi. My son walks in very slowly, his head hung low. I leap over to him.

"Son, are you okay?"

"They beat me, Mom. They took my shoes off and beat the bottom of my feet. All up and down my legs and back," he growls, slightly gritting his teeth, his eyes red and teary.

I glare over at the police officer. "You beat my son?!" I scream.

"No, we didn't," the officer blatantly lies.

"He just told me you did." I scowl.

Then just as the words are shooting out of my mouth, I glance over and see a man's footprint on the back of Shedi's white T-shirt. The print is just below his neck, to the left side of the shoulder blades. I scream again while pointing at the print, "What the hell is this if you didn't beat him? Where did this footprint come from?"

The officer continues denying. "We didn't touch him."

"You are lying! Look at his shirt! There's a footprint right there! I want to speak to the chief of the police department right now! Call him right now!" The neighbor that came with me finally speaks up and tells the officer that he needs to get the chief of police down there immediately.

The officer makes some phone calls and informs me that the chief is on his way. We wait for another hour, still no chief. Again, I begin demanding. Finally, after another fifteen minutes, the chief shows up at the police station. We discuss what's happened—very loudly. The man tells me to write a formal complaint against the four officers who beat my son. I calmly review the details with Shedi and write them all out by hand— officially filing a case against those involved. We finally leave the station.

I sit in the back seat of the car and cry all the way home. I have disconnected from the world around me. All I can see is my son's face as they push him into the wagon. All I can hear is his phone call repeating over and over in my mind—*"They're beating me."*

When we arrive at the house, he shows me the marks on his feet, up and down his back legs and buttocks.

"We're going to the hospital right now," I insist. "We have to get this documented."

We go to one of the nearest hospitals and I explain what the police have done to my son. They ask us to have a seat. We wait, and wait, and wait. We're never served. The nurses keep feeding me lies to pacify my anger. We wait two more hours. Without giving any reason at all, they finally tell us that they can't help me.

"Okay, I'll go to another hospital then," I bark at the nurse as I storm out of the room.

Again, we enter another hospital. Again, I explain what's happened. Again, we're put off like the last one. As the minutes go by, I become more and more enraged and disgusted. They keep telling me that the doctor is coming in, but he doesn't. We dance around like this for three more hours.

Suddenly, I belt out in disgust, "Are you people insane? What are you trying to tell me? That you're scared of the police or something?" They stand frozen like stone just staring at me.

Finally, one of the doctors comes over to me, leans in closely and says, "Yes, we are. We can't do a report against the police. I'm sorry."

My son finally speaks out: "Forget these guys, Mom. Let's just go home."

We leave empty handed. I feel like I've failed my son again. For the next three days, I can't stop the tears. I cannot accept what has happened to Shedi.

I finally tell Shedi, "Maybe I should go to the embassy and tell them what has happened." Apparently, as I am contemplating going to the American Embassy, the police are at the station worrying I just might do something like that. They're scavenging about, trying to think of a way to get out of this crisis.

The next day, the Chief of Police comes to my home with the four men who beat Shedi to give us a formal apology. They tell me that in return for my forgiveness of this incident, my son and I can have free reign of the city.

"Both of you will be given a special pass, and it will let any police officer know to not bother you at all—ever again." His apologetic smile is nauseating to me.

At first, I am irate. I feel like they're just trying to bribe me. I don't know what to do. What they've done is unforgivable, but my neighbor soon becomes the voice of reason in this maddening situation.

He offers me sound advice. "Yasmine, you're better off making friends, than making enemies.

I gravely weigh the situation. I choose to forgive the men and accept the free passes for Shedi and me. Both parties sign a truce contract.

After this incident, Sultan Azam Temuri, Senior Superintendent of the Islamabad Traffic Police invited me to join the Civilian Human Rights Board. Accepting this invitation meant that I could visit the different jails throughout Islamabad and the neighboring cities and check for human rights violations before reporting to the board about any issues that needed attention. I graciously accepted and took my new opportunity very seriously. Going into the jails and requesting changes was not only the scariest thing that I have ever done, but one of the most rewarding as well.

I quickly became a regular at police headquarters. I offered and taught English to Islamabad traffic police officers several times a week. My goal was to help the local traffic police officers communicate better with English-speaking visitors—hopefully preventing another incident like me son's. My students were scattered throughout the city. Whenever they recognized me as I drove by, they would salute me on the spot.

I'd also do was volunteer for many different projects around the city. The most fun of them being the Seat Belt Awareness Campaigns where I'd literally stand at different intersections around town for hours—talking to folks in their cars while the traffic light was red—asking them to buckle up.

"Hi." I'd say with a huge smile, and donning my florescent yellow vest. "How are you today? Can I ask you to put your seat belt on please? Thanks. Remember, seat belts save lives!"

All of these programs combined served as a much-needed catalyst for my inner healing and forgiveness. Because of my public position, It wasn't uncommon for me to somehow appear in the newspapers once a week or so. One day a friend of mine popped into my office to check on me.

"Yasmine, are you okay?"

"Yeah, I'm great. Why?"

"I haven't seen you in the paper in a couple of weeks. "

(Me (left), Superintendent Termuri (middle) at a police function. This is definitely not one of my most photogenic moments.)

(Me (far left) wearing my yellow vest at a Seat Belt Awareness Campaign
Rally. I was talking to Nudul.)

(Me (center) and Mona (far right) volunteering on a Disabled Citizen
Safety Campaign.)

Mr. Rizvi

Shedi had returned to the States again, and with time, my charitable work extended far beyond the Islamabad police department. For instance, I had the opportunity to work for an amazing humanitarian in Islamabad in early 2000's—the Honorable Syed Zia U. Rizvi, Former Assistant Secretary General United Nations and Director General Independent Bureau for Humanitarian Issues (known as IBHI)—serving as his personal assistant for about 8 months. He is pure-hearted and an endless wealth of humanitarian knowledge. This opportunity helped fulfill a lifelong dream of working for the United Nations (even if it was in a round-about-sort-of-way).

Sadly, though, my dream came to an end. I had to resign because he needed me to travel to the States with him on official United Nation business—which I couldn't do for obvious reasons. Nevertheless, I will always cherish the time we spent together and those lengthy in-depth discussions about UN politics, and various humanitarian issues around the world, and possible solutions for them. He was even generous enough to instate me on as one of the Board of Directors of IBHI.

During our brief time together, I learnt a myriad of things from Mr. Rizvi, for example, how to help those whom have been displaced within their own country, or how to use military forces in times of natural disasters. However, oddly enough, the most bewildering skill that I acquired from him was the art of *shoe reading*. He taught me that by observing a person's shoes I could home in on their personality instantly—thus knowing what type of person that I was dealing with. For instance, a man who has refined or sophisticated ways tends to wear pointed-toe shoes, whereas a man who's more humble or family-oriented tends to wear squared-toed shoes.

Tried and tested, he was a hundred percent correct about it and I still use this practice today. So, don't be surprised if we meet one day, and I happen to glance downwards—because you will know what I'm most likely doing.

Heaven or Hell?

It's a lazy morning on October 8, 2005. I'm asleep on my bed, face down with Nudul crawling around me. The bed begins rocking back and forth. The dish showcase begins to rattle.

"Nudul. Calm down, baby. You're shaking the whole bed," I mumble.

Then, I realize that the bed is *still* shaking, and the dishes are *still* rattling. It's an earthquake! I jump up and whisk Nudul to the front door with me. Mona dashes out of her room and joins us in the doorway. We stand together in fear. The room jerks back and forth for what seems like two minutes. It stops, but the building still echoes movement for a few seconds. We remain still for a brief moment. All goes quiet and the kids resume what they were doing. Since I've just woken up, I go straight to the bathroom. I drop my pants and sit on the toilet. I'm not even finished when a second earthquake hits—this time much stronger than the first. I grab my pants, run out of the bathroom, and return to the doorway. The kids have already made their way back and assumed position. The room continues to jerk back and forth.

Finally, the jerking stops again. We linger at the door a bit longer this time before disbursing. This second jolt has clearly shaken us up. I feel unnerved. Suddenly, the phone rings. It's my laptop friend from Dunkin' Donuts.

"Yasmine, are you okay? Did you feel that?" he says anxiously.

"Yeah, that was a big one. The second one was much bigger than the first. Did you notice that?"

"Yeah! You're right!" he says. I hear some mumbling on his end of the phone in the background. Then suddenly he screeches, "Oh no!"

"What?"

"Someone just called my brother and said that one side of Margalla Tower fell down."

"What? Are you serious? The apartments by my house, right?"

"Yeah, it just fell down. Oh man, I gotta go."

"Yeah, okay. Oh no, I can't believe …" I'm still uttering words as he hangs up the phone. I dash to my patio in the front of my apartment to see for myself. I look out in horror. He's right; the building is gone. I can no longer see it from my house. A chill goes up my spine. I almost rented an apartment there—in that very building. I can't believe it's just *gone*—ten stories high, and now… just gone.

About twenty minutes go by; another call comes in.

"Hello?" I say, still clearly shaken up.

"Yasmine, are you okay?" I quickly recognize as the voice of the translator from the American Embassy (the one who came for the welfare checks of the kids in Kalu).

"Yeah, uncle, I'm okay."

"Oh, thank God." He sighs in relief. "I was thinking that you were living in the Margalla apartments."

"No…. Yeah…. Well, I'd looked at them, but decided not to. But I can see the apartments from my house. It's gone."

The building came down during the second quake. I probably didn't hear it because I was in the bathroom. I'm traumatized. When I finally turn on the news all of the channels are covering the tragedy. I can see one of my friends, a doctor—he's atop of the cement rubble—trying to rescue those inside. My spirit inside me is unsettled. Something is haunting me, and I'm drawn to the site. I decide I have to go there. When I arrive, I just stand on the sidelines, watching the frantic men work on the debris mass. It's total chaos around me. People are in the streets crying and walking around in a daze.

I see this thin, older white man, walking back and forth. He looks disoriented. He is calling a woman's name over and over. He tells the person next to me that his wife is still in the basement.

The earthquake affected everyone in Pakistan that day. Thousands of people were killed. Everyone was somehow connected to the tragedy.

The epicenter of the 7.6 magnitude earthquake was in Muzaffarabad—further north in Pakistan, about an hour away from Islamabad. A local radio station covering the disaster invited me to go along and I accepted.

I was in awe as I rode in the mini-van—packed with reporters and recording gear. No words can explain how majestic the mountainous areas in that region are. We stopped the vehicle at one end of the valley and looked down the middle. You could see greened mountains on each side of the canyon, cascading into infinity. The morning view had a lovely foggy effect to it. It truly looked like some scenic view that you would find on a travel brochure. *Breathtaking!*

This heavenly view was soon marred with tears and terror as we inched closer and closer to what could only be described as Hell on Earth. We came upon several small villages along the mountainside that had been destroyed by the quake. Entire families were buried under the rubble of houses. Water supplies were out. Families were displaced, cold, and hungry. We came upon one man sitting atop a mountain of debris that was once his home. He stared straight ahead in utter silence. His entire family was buried under the cement layer. He had no way to get them out. He'd lost his wife, his mother, and his four children—all of whom were in the home at the time the quake hit.

We then came upon a village that the military had not yet found to assist. Villagers were grabbing at my arms as we walked down the road, begging for food and blankets. The devastation and human tragedy was too much for me. I could take no more. I went back to the van, sat alone and cried. I wanted to go home. I was utterly useless and unable to help these hurting people.

Our final stop on the tour was a hospital where the injured were being transported. One of the hospital interns took us around to show us the damage in the footings of the hospital and to explain the types of casualties that had been coming in from all over the disaster area.

"See this woman here? She's dying. Look at the way she's breathing. She's gasping for air. We have so many patients and not enough room or supplies for them all," the young doctor explained. He led us outside the hospital, to several green army tents that were set up to accommodate the overflow. It resembled a war zone.

These disturbing scenes of human calamity are forever etched in my mind. They say that over eighty thousand people died because of that day. I was spared, but only God knows why.

Run!

It's a beautiful spring day in 2007. Mona and I are on mother-daughter shopping trip—for shoes—in the F-8 area of Islamabad. We park in front of our favorite shoe store and head inside. We begin browsing around. Suddenly I start hearing a long steady hissing sound.

SSSSSSSSSSSSSSSSSSSSSSSSSSSSSSSSSSSSS.

It's loud, continuous, and extremely unusual. *Hey, what's that noise?* I glance over at the entrance door with curiosity, but I don't see anything strange, so I turn back around and continue our shoe hunt. All the while, I can still hear the hissing in the background.

About thirty seconds go by and the hissing is not getting any weaker.

"What is that?" I say with annoyance.

I glance over at the main door again and see that several men are starting to gather just outside the door. They too are looking, trying to see where the hissing sound is coming from. Suddenly, as I try to look over the men, there's an explosion across the street at a gas station. A wall of flames shoots about two hundred feet into the sky. Within seconds, a shockwave of vibration comes towards us, and the entire building shakes.

I grab my daughter and run outside. I don't know if we're having airstrikes or what. All I know is I want to run.

We run out the door and off to the right. Two stores down, I stop to gather my thoughts. "What do I do?" I scream.

I pull out my cell phone and call the Superintendent of Traffic Police, Termuri. His housemaid answers the phone.

"Hello?" she says.

"Is Termuri there?" I request abruptly.

"He's busy right now," she answers not knowing the gravity of the situation.

"Get him on the phone! I need to talk to him right now," I demand.

Again, she refuses. "He is busy right now."

"This is an emergency! Get him on the phone right now!" I scream. I hear a shuffle of the phone. I can tell that she is passing it to someone else. I hear my muffled name. My heart is racing from fear, but now I'm getting angry too.

"Oh, just get him on the phone. Hello?" I bark out.

"Hi, Yasmine," he says pleasantly.

Without any hesitation, I yell, "The gas station's blown up!"

"Where are you?" Suddenly he understands the significance of my call.

"I'm in F-8 and the gas station just blew up! I don't know how many people are dead."

"Okay. We're coming."

"Finally!" I flip the phone shut only for a second blast to occur, this one seeming bigger than the first. This time, I don't stand there to look at the wall of flames; I grab my daughter's arm and we start running for our lives. I'm so confused, and I don't know where to go. *Are we being attacked? Where do I go?*

It's total chaos. People are dashing to and fro. I keep running along the cement path until we reach the back of the mall. It seems to be a good enough distance to give me some time to think of what to do next.

I stand on the veranda walkway, crying and gripping Mona's hand. We're both shaking and scared. A concerned woman sees us and comes out to invite us into her store to hide. Life is a sudden blur. I'm breathing so hard—terrified out of my wits. For twenty minutes, we stand in the store with the woman. We can hear people saying outside two storage cylinders at the natural gas station have blown up. The fire and police are now working on it.

An hour later, I finally have the nerve to go see my car. The fire is contained so all is clear. We're relieved to get out of there safely.

The next day, the local news reported that one of the natural gas main cylinders was leaking from the main valve—thus, the long eerie hissing noise. They also added that an idiot with a cigarette had caused the explosion but luckily there were no fatalities. For months afterwards, I was traumatized. My heart raced each time I pulled in to get gas. Not an easy thing to forget.

I Am An American!

We lived in Pakistan with expired passports for many years, essentially living as illegal aliens. In 2002, since all three of our passports had expired, I went ahead and applied for mine and Mona's passport as well, along with Shedi. He left with his emergency passport, and the American Embassy gave us Mona's passport with no problems. However, apparently, renewing *mine* was a different story. Whenever I called to inquire about it, they'd tell me that they had my application, but that they'd lost my passport and that they were *trying* to find it. I highly doubted their story.

By 2006, I still had received no documentation. I felt like I'd been abandoned. I had tried everything to get my passport from them; including writing a letter to an Arizona Senator asking for his help. But he returned an answer saying he was sorry, but, there was nothing that he could do for me.

At my wit's end, I finally decided enough was enough. *I'm an American, and I have a right to my passport. They can't take that away from me and just leave me here with no papers.*

So, I picked up the phone and called the same man from the embassy that I had been dealing with about my passport issue for years.

"I can't take anymore. I'm going public with my story. I'll call the news and tell them that for some reason I haven't gotten my passport for the last four years from your office."

In a flat monotone voice he replied, "We're still looking for it." He was not apologetic at all.

Again, I felt as if my phone call to the American Embassy was a waste of time. I still had no clue as to where my passport was, but I needed it, if I were ever to leave Pakistan.

Less than twenty-four hours later, I received a surprising phone call. "Yasmine, we've found your passport."

"Oh, really? How surprising," I say with clear sarcasm while thrusting my hand up in the air in victory.

"Yes. You can come down first thing tomorrow morning and get it."

"I'll be there." *Finally!*

I knew it was risky; but I needed that little blue book. I began to think about the what-ifs? *What if they arrest me inside the embassy? What if I don't come out?* Being worried about the kids, I called up Zain's family with instructions of what to do in case things went awry. Most importantly, if they didn't get a phone call from me by one p.m.—that meant that they needed to come to Islamabad.

The next morning came much faster than usual. All night long, I lay awake worrying. I was downright scared. This is how my morning went.

∗∗∗

I get up early to ensure that I'm not late, and when I reach the allocated parking lot, I leave my purse hidden in the car. There's no point in taking it inside; they'll just rummage through everything and take whatever they feel could be dangerous. Plus, there are no cell phones allowed anyway, so why bother? It's just easier to leave these things behind and only take my Pakistani government-issued ID card.

I stand in several lines, one after another. It's quite ironic, actually; most of the people around me are trying to get their visa to go to America—the one place I can't go. The lines move smoothly and I finally receive a pass that enables me to enter the main embassy building. I find a seat in the crowded veranda. I'm nervous just thinking what is about to happen or what could happen. I decide to get some juice from the small snack shop that's attached to the veranda. Once I have my snack, I take my seat on a wooden bench and fretfully wait for someone to call my name. I look around and see a variety of applicants—young and old alike. One young couple goes up to the window and receives the news that the wife's visa has been approved. Such joy is evident on her face.

Finally, a man's voice calls out my name. I muster the courage to get up and push forward. When I approach the window, the man tells me to go into the office door to the left. I see one man behind him looking at me. My heart skips a beat. Maybe I'm just paranoid. I step cautiously into the brown, dimmed room. It feels like I'm heading into the lion's den.

The room is only about twenty feet by twenty feet square. The wall in the back of the small room has a counter built in with security glass to separate us. There's a man in a suit standing directly in the center of the window. Four other people stand behind him in a crescent formation. I think to myself, *This is it. They're going to trap me. Why else would it take five people to give one woman a passport?*My legs feel weak. All of them have a serious look on their faces. I walk to the window frightened like a stray cat; my eyes are wide open, and I'm ready to flee at the slightest scent of danger. I reach the counter and see a passport in the man's hand, held with a firm grip.

The man lays the document on the counter and begins sliding it under the security glass towards me.

In a firm voice, he says, "Marsha, we're going to give you your passport today, but..." Mid-sentence, he stops pushing the passport forward—just as it reaches the security glass—and pauses—as though trying to entice me. I warily stretch my hand to take it from him, but he's not releasing it. He continues with forewarning in his voice, looking me dead in the eye. "...if you try to enter the States at any point of entry, you *will* be captured. Do you understand?" The steadiness and careful grouping of his words make the consequences impossible to misconstrue.

"Yes—yes, I understand." My voice trembles and crackles with a clashing of fear and confidence. He withdraws his hand from the blue book, and I pull it inward. As I pick my passport up, I feel an indescribable sense of victory. I've been without a sense of belonging for so many years. I now have proof of who I am. I am an American! I look up at the embassy officials with tears swelling up in my eyes. "Thank you," I say with all sincerity.

"Goodbye, Marsha," the man says.

"Goodbye." I turn and walk out of the lion's den. I head towards the exit with my passport in hand. I contain myself from leaping for joy as I twirl through the metal exit gate. I rush back to my car as fast as I can.

I pull out my cell phone and call the family. "All is well. I've made it out. It's finally finished. I have my passport."

(My favorite picture of my mommy.)

My Greatest Loss

It's a crisp night in 2006. I've just finished some light grocery shopping on my way home from work. I'm settling down in the driver's seat and hear that I've just received a text message. I pull out my phone. The message is from my stepfather, Cliffy. I am stunned.

Marsha, your mother passed away peacefully in her sleep last night.

***

Suddenly, I'm a child again.
My balloon is adrift.
My hand is empty.
My heart is broken.
I cry.

***

I still cry. I love you Mom. I miss you so much.

Unlikely Visitor

Soon after the 2006 earthquake that rocked Northern Pakistan, I get some interesting news. Zain calls me out of the blue and says, "Hey, Yasmine. I'm coming home for good."

"What? Are you serious?" I can't believe what I'm hearing.

"Yeah. Something's come up here; I'll explain it to you later. Anyway, I'll be there in three days. Pick me up at the airport." He sounds very direct, and I'm totally confused.

"Okay, okay. See you in three days." I hang up the phone. My legs have gone weak. His words echo through my mind. Coming home to *me*? For good? After all of these years—really? I honestly never thought he'd leave the States.

It takes a few minutes for his news to really sink in, and suddenly it hits me.

"Wait! In three days!?"

My mind scurries about. I begin mumbling to myself. *He'll be here in three days? What, forever? Wait! What am I going to do now? I don't love him anymore. And what about his fiancé, or girlfriend, or wife or* whatever *she is? What happened to her? Does he really think that I've just forgotten all of that?*

We're still legally married according to Pakistani law, and obviously still married in his mind, too. After pacing for what seems to be the full three days, I decide to be honest with him right when I pick him up at the airport. When I see him standing there in the terminal, I walk straight up to him and extend my hand to shake. He's clearly shaken up about something—most likely whatever caused him to return to Pakistan for good. We exchange pleasantries and leave the terminal together.

I eventually start the conversation. It feels awkward, but I know I have to do it.

"Umm, yeah, you see, here's the thing; I understand that we're married, and we can live together—no problem—but, umm, that's it. We're not husband and wife anymore—in that sense of the word. I don't want anything to do with that part of it. Okay?"

Zain didn't take too well to our new living arrangement. He was angry and I knew it. He began arguing with me every day, each episode increasing in intensity and vulgarity. The breaking point came the day he changed routes while driving and took me to a deserted area, parked the car, and began blaring at me. I cowered in the back seat and terrified—crying and praying to God that he didn't snap.

Within the next few days, I tried dropping the idea of divorce, but things swiftly got out of control.

***

I'm folding laundry in our bedroom when I somehow convince myself that now is a good time to speak up.

"Things have been kind of rough since you got back. I know you're unhappy. Maybe we should divorce, so that *you* can go ahead and remarry—you know, start a new family?" I offer with fake confidence.

Suddenly he lunges across the room and pins me against the wall, his hand across my neck. I can't breathe.

"I will never divorce you," he growls at me. The force of his anger explodes onto my face. I close my eyes in fear. "Do you understand me? I will kill you first. Do you understand? No divorce! Ever!"

"Okay—okay. No divorce," I barely choke out. I *have* to agree with him so that he will let me go.

The next morning, he thinks that I'm okay; but I'm not. I just can't let this happen to me again. I have to tell someone this time. As soon as I'm able leave home, I head straight to the police station and file a report. The police officers come home with me and stay as I pack our stuff and move to a safe house at the police station.

I'd lost another marriage to domestic abuse. Again, I was on my own, with absolutely no financial fallback. There was no one to depend on except myself. I was absolutely on my own. All I had were my two children, my English language, and my accent-training job. It didn't pay much, but I was diligent and stayed positive.

Soon, my patience paid off. It wasn't too long afterwards that I was sent to go meet with the Dean of Bahria University about a social function being planned on behalf of the Islamabad Traffic Police. The dean and I sat in his office for a half-an-hour chatting about various details, when suddenly out of nowhere he announced, "You're going to work for me here in the English Department. You are not leaving my office today without signing a job contract."

"Me?" I said. "I'm going to be working for the university?" I was dumbfounded. *Where did all of this come from? How can I work here? I don't have a degree or anything—this can't be happening.*

But just as the dean had prophesied, within an hour I had a job offer in my hand with a starting date. My hand was literally shaking while signing the papers. I just couldn't believe it. We'd just met, and yet he'd hired me on the spot to create a communication lab for the bachelor's program. It was the opportunity of a lifetime. I'd expanded my career and boosted my salary by three hundred percent in one simple meeting. It was the *exact miracle* that I'd needed at that time.

Celebrities

During the many years abroad, I was fortunate enough to have met many famous entertainment legends including Abida Parveen, Javed Aktar, Shabana Azmi, Brian Lara, Shafqat Amanat Ali, RDB, Atif Aslam, Rabbi Shergill, Annie, and Cricketers Inzamam-ul-Haq, Mohammad Yousuf and Brian Lara. I met these amazing people at a variety of venues—concerts, weddings, plays and restaurants. While meeting them at weddings and plays was fairly easy, concerts presented a bit more of a challenge. In order to get backstage, I'd have to create extravagant stories, like claiming to be a press agent from the local news channel, or pretending that I'd just traveled all the way from America for that particular concert and therefore denying my entrance would be downright cruel.

Each of these meeting holds a special memory in my heart; like the time Abida Parveen hugged me after her performance at a wedding. And the time I met Atif Aslam at his car while it was pouring down rain and then went out for coffee with him and his crew afterwards. And the time when the extremely congenial Shahbana Azmi insisted on taking a picture with Mona and me, and then took another one with her husband, the legendary poet Javed Aktar. It's impossible to say which opportunity was the most impressive. But I can this for sure, that I was thrilled beyond words when Shafqat Amanat Ali dedicated his famous song *Mitwa* to his "new friend Yasmine" during his concert in Islamabad in which we first met.

Then, there was this amazing day when I accidentally tagged along with Sultan Hassanal Bolkiahand and his lovely wife during a museum tour in Islamabad—*without* any made-up stories by the way—it was purely by accident. It was sometime in 2007, and I just happened to be visiting the city museum that day. I walked up the front walkway just a few steps behind a group of about eight people, not thinking anything of it at the time. I did, however, notice that the two people in the front of the group were receiving quite special attention from the museum employees. They were smiling and fussing all over them. I patiently waited for the group to move along—still not knowing who they were. Soon, they began a tour the museum.

Cool, a tour, I thought. *Since, I'm alone today I'll just go ahead and tag along.*

The funny thing is that no one even questioned me about it or asked me to back off; I can only assume that everyone thought I was *with* the dignitaries. After a while, still noticing that the two in the front were really getting the *royal treatment*, I whispered to a lady whom I had been walking next to for a while, "And who *are* those two people in the front?"

She smiled and said, "The King and Queen of Brunei."

"Really? Awesome!" I said slightly under my breath—making sure to walk calmly—so as not to blow my stealthy position in the group. As we walked, I chatted with the king's personal assistant. I asked all kinds of questions about her country, Brunei, and she was kind enough to answer them all. She even gave me her email address so we could keep in touch. Overall, it was a splendid tour and a wonderfully surprising day indeed. And yes—the king and queen just happened to look over at me—one time. I can't help but wonder what they must've been thinking when they saw me with their posse.

Probably, something like, *who's that white chick?*

***

Conversely, in a way, I'd reached my own celebrity status in Islamabad. Not only through all of my police work, but with the help of GEO TV.

175

They'd filmed a short documentary news-piece in Kalu about me living in the village for all of those years. They had me do such cheesy things like sweep the floor, hang laundry, and pull turnips out of the ground in the fields. They even interviewed members of my Zain's family. I'd already moved to Islamabad, and was actually with my class—at work—during the first time that it aired. My class and I stood watching and laughing. It was hilarious! They played it every half hour for a day or two. So much so, that I was recognized around town afterwards.

I would hear things like this: "Hey-y, aren't you that *gori* on TV from the village?" I'd admit it, and then the questions about my entire life would continue for the next hour or so.

I was also known for some of the radio commercials I did for one of the popular pop stations. It was so cool to walk into a mall and hear my commercial playing over the sound system. I'd often have people compliment me about my voice when they realized that it was me. One day, while I was shopping in a little side shop, my commercial came on right as the man was helping me. I looked at the little AM radio, then looked at him. He had absolutely no idea that it was me. I couldn't help but giggle; it was just amusing to me.

Most Embarrassing Moment Award

(And now, may I have the envelope, please?
<Insert drum roll sound effect.>)

I have lots and lots of things to be embarrassed about. But the award for *Most Embarrassing Moment* goes to the time I was working at Bahria University as Head of the Communication Lab. I was brand new on the faculty and was just learning how things worked around administration. Overall, it was a great feeling to be part of such an esteemed institution. And when I received my first salary deposit, I was pleasantly surprised by the amount. My salary was *far more* than I had expected. In fact, it had *quadrupled!* I remember thinking, *Did I misunderstand exactly how much I will be making? Hmm? Oh well, let's go shopping!* So, like an idiot, instead of double-checking the deposit for any errors, I spent it all.

Three months had gone by, and I was living it up—I thought I'd finally found my gravy train. Until one day, I got called into the chancellor's office. When I arrived, there were already two other men from accounting sitting with him. I nervously walked in and joined them. The air was still, and by the somber looks on their faces, I instantly knew that something was wrong, but I was not ready for what came next.

The chancellor began, "Ms. Yasmine, we're so sorry, but we realize that a major mistake on our part has happened. You've been receiving double pay since you started with us here at the university and we just realized it. Again, we're truly sorry about any inconvenience, but we need the money back as soon as possible."

I was dumbfounded. I just sat silent (for what seemed an hour). *Money? What money? Oh no! What am I going to do now?* I tried to explain to them, "Sir,

I am sorry, but I had no idea, and I've already spent the money." I began stammering. "This-s is not my fault. I don't *have* it to give back right now, do I? Please sir, I need time to save it up."

The chancellor spoke up sharply, "Ms. Yasmine. I am sorry, but if you do not return the money in a week's time, we will have to call the police and file a report."

His words struck me like lightning. The other two men sat in silence, peering straight at me. It was clear that they were not even going to try to save me.

What a change of tide—I was in quite a pickle.

I left the office grief-stricken. I had no idea what I was going to do. Three months of double-salary was gone. I urgently sought the advice of my close friend and Head Librarian, Amin.

"Didn't you realize that you were being paid double?" he asked.

"Uhh, no! If I had, I wouldn't be in this situation right now, would I?"

Together we tried to think of a solution. It was an unnerving situation. Despite everything, I kept up with my normal routine at the university for the next couple of days, but internally I was constantly brooding about the money. Amin tried to keep my spirits up the best he could. We had tea together in his office, several times a day while throwing around some ideas. A few days later, he had some work at a neighboring university, and asked me to come along with—giving us even more time to think. Time was quickly running out and no answer was in sight. The change of scenery at the different university still couldn't sway my mood. We entered his friend's office and they began chatting instantly; I don't remember what they were yapping about, because—quite frankly—I had my own problems. Suddenly, Amin's friend asked him why I was so down. Looking to me for approval, Amin began explaining in detail what had happened with my salary issue at our university. I was so ashamed at how completely incompetent I must've looked in their eyes that I gazed downward and kept my silence.

But, you will not believe what happened next.

Without saying a word, the man pulled out his personal checkbook and asked how much money I needed to pay back. Understanding what he was about to do, Amin and I just looked at each other—dazed.

"Oh, no, I can't..." I started.

He stopped me mid-sentence. "How much do you owe them?" He had such compassion in his eyes and absolutely no judgment. I felt as if I were dreaming. He wrote out the check for the exact amount that I needed, and slid it across the table to me. He continued in a humble tone. "The only thing I ask of you is that you don't tell anyone about this. You can pay me back whenever it is comfortable for you."

Once again, God provided for me when I needed it most. It took me over a year to pay the money back, but this Angel of Mercy never once asked about it. Still today, I'm keeping my promise—by not mentioning his name—and I pray for him always.

Time to Return

Working at the university was an amazing privilege and experience—both socially and professionally. That *is* once I got past the salary drama. Many things happened during the next year-and-a-half of my life—good and bad. The most painful moment occurred when Zain decided that Nudul belonged with him in the village. He took him away—not giving me any choice in the matter. I begged and pleaded with him to return my son, but my pleas were only met with more anger and threats. There was no way that I could win this issue in court, and I knew it.

Broken-hearted without Nudul, I pressed on—one day at a time. I had no choice. It was down to just Mona and me. Not long after, I grew very close to a Pakistani colleague of mine. His name was Adi; he was eighteen years my junior. We'd been dating for quite a while when a close friend of ours *suggested* that our union would be good for *me*, citing a saying in the East that goes: "It is better for a woman to stand in the shade of a tree than to stand in the sun alone."

We got married in secret. The only people who knew were my children and two mutual friends who were sworn to silence. Adi insisted that no one was allowed to know about us. Not our co-workers. Not his family. Not even any of his closest buddies. Pathetically, I fell for all of his ridiculous excuses and reasoning; even to the point of living separately—I lived two houses down from his parents, and he'd come and go as he wished. Honestly, any movie company could easily write a melodrama based on this particular relationship alone. Our secret union was in constant turmoil. I'd fallen in love with him, but his feelings for me and our marriage were obviously something totally different. I just wish I'd seen it much sooner.

Two months after we married, I wanted to move to Dubai (in the United Arab Emirates) because the political situation in Pakistan was becoming too unstable. It was 2008, and I was offered an English teaching job at a college in Al Ain, UAE. Adi couldn't make up his mind about whether he would go with me or not. He insisted that it wasn't easy to leave his family behind. I was frustrated with him and the whole me vs. his family ordeal. I couldn't wait on him any longer. I was leaving Pakistan—with or without him. He finally mustered the courage to tell his parents that he was leaving Pakistan to *find work*. (Yes, you read it correctly. He was leaving to *find work*, not to be *my husband*. Did I mention my knack for making bad decisions yet?)

Our secret marriage finally surfaced after about six months in the UAE. His parents were irate about it and refused to speak to him afterwards for several months. I sincerely felt sorry for him about that, but his family was never close with me anyway so their silent treatment didn't sting me at all. Yet, now that the cat was out of the bag, I actually thought that we'd be able to start living a normal married life together—freeing me to talk about it publicly—but I was wrong. I still had to be a silent partner as Adi kept me from the rest of his family that still didn't know about me. He had his Facebook page and I had mine—both with a single relationship status on them. One time, I posted a picture of us together on my profile and he went totally ballistic on me. Honestly, I just couldn't understand why he wanted to keep our marriage so buried, but I went along with it anyway.

Then, one morning, he got up and announced to me that he was leaving for Pakistan. He said that he was going to go speak to his parents in person about accepting me and a possible reconciliation within the family. At first, I was angry that he'd arranged such an important trip without my consent, but I still held on to hope that this idea might work and that his family would finally come around. But again, he was lying. I found out that he had really gone home to marry his cousin. The blow was devastating—I fell on the floor and cried for hours.

Two weeks later, he called me on the phone and begged forgiveness, saying that I just didn't understand his obligation to his family's wishes. Knowing that I was already on marriage number three, I didn't want to give up so easily. I let him come back. He was only gone to Pakistan for a month; his new bride was living with his family there. Again, I fell for his lies hook, line, and sinker.

Believe it or not, I really tried to live with this arrangement for about a year, but, in doing so, I became clinically depressed. I cried profusely all the time, and felt that my life was not worth living anymore. Thankfully, I sought help from a doctor. She prescribed depression medicine to help me *"adjust and accept my new arrangement,"* but it turned me into a vegetable. I had so much pain and rage inside, but the meds kept me silent and in line. It was as if I was living in some kind of plastic bubble, watching life from the inside. All of my pain was the same, but my voice couldn't reach the outer world.

I was watching Adi play out his deception each day. He'd receive missed calls and text messages from Wife Number Two during the night. Then, during the day, he'd leave home to go call her privately—keeping his secret intact. (Only God knows what he was telling her.) I kept telling myself that she was the victim too. His lying was not her fault, but my emotions had become a melting pot of anger and jealousy—molten lava waiting to erupt.

One day, I just couldn't take any more of my vegetative state and the double-life that he was leading. I stopped taking my medication, without consulting the doctor—cold turkey. I figured that life was better when I could express myself—if we were to fight again—then so be it. As a result of stopping the meds, I suffered withdrawals for about week. It was so strange, like someone was inside my head, flipping a light switch on and off. Electric pulses would shoot through my body—even down to my fingertips. It wasn't painful, but it was uncomfortable because I felt like my nervous system was disconnected.

As soon as my old-self returned, I spilled the beans to wife number two. Within a week, she left him and asked for divorce. Then, to top it all off, I got the blame from the family for ruining *their* lives. (Go figure.)

Overall, we actually managed to drag this disastrous marriage out for about seven years—it was the ultimate emotional pit. He finally admitted to me that he'd married me out of charity. Again, I'd let someone abuse me—but on a whole new level. I finally accepted that it was time to end it. I'd let it go on for far too long. Yep, this was divorce number three. Not proud of it, but it is what it is. I own it.

Even after my third divorce, I received even more marriage proposals.

"Oh God, are you serious?" I'd immediately snap back. "No, thank you. I've had enough of that crap to last me three lifetimes."

As I mentioned earlier, I saw a doctor for my depression. During our sessions, I'd cry profusely; not only about the marital issues but also, also about some serious concerns I had about my daughter, Mona. I knew she'd always been particularly different from the rest, but I just didn't understand how or why. All I knew was that she hadn't developing socially as other children her age. Truth be told, deep down, I blamed myself. I thought that my raising her outside America had somehow messed her up. Finally, one day, my doctor asked me to bring her in so she could meet with her in order to understand her exact symptoms. It took only one meeting for the doctor to recognize the issue.

"Your daughter is autistic, and appears to have some learning differences," she explained. "Yasmine, you've been carrying this guilt around for so many years. You need to let that go. Your daughter needs you right now, and she needs the attention from specialized programs in her native country. You really should take her back to the States. What if something happens to you here?"

I was blind-sided with her diagnosis. These terms were unfamiliar to me, but I began reading as much as I could about autism, which only solidified that the doctor was correct in her views. Her advice remained dormant in the back of my mind for another year. But when the sickening Adi drama ended, I finally started seeing things more clearly. I began pondering what would happen to Mona if I died. *She has no one here. She'll be alone and scared. She can't work; how will she take care of herself? Who will take care of her?* These thoughts weighed on my heart daily.

Overall, Mona and I had been quite happy in UAE; we loved it so much. I had a lucrative teaching jobs, amazing students, lots of friends scattered throughout several countries. There was so much to do and see. But, deep down, I knew I was avoiding the truth. I knew Mona needed to go back to build her life in America and get special training, and I didn't want her to have to do it without me. Even if that meant I'd be in a jail close to her, at least she'd know I was there. Shedi was in America, working and stable; he'd be able to take care of his sister just in case I did end up in jail. It seemed like perfect timing.

My heart assured me that it was the time for change. Time to go back home. Time to clear my name once and for all. Time to stop running and let past wounds heal. Time to mend the broken relationships between the kids and their father. But the only way to do any of that was to put myself in the most vulnerable position—to surrender to the authorities. It was the only answer, and I knew it.

Of course, to do this would take careful planning. I made a list of all the things that I needed and wanted to do. The list was extensive, but now I had a goal: return to America. Eventually, my list consisted of:

- Hire an attorney and set my surrender in motion.
- Pool all of my monetary resources together and purchase a business for the family. (Owner our own business would give us a good foundation in America. And, I'd know I'd have a job waiting when I got there. We could pay the money back from there.)
- Have Shedi find us an apartment. Send a year's worth of rent so Mona will be settled—just in case I go to jail.
- Send money for beds, food, and a car.
- Have some clothes altered. Take three inches off my maxi skirts.
- Pack up all of our special belongings that we've collected over the years and ship them overseas. Buy the boxes to pack them in.
- Buy the tickets.
- Buy a year's worth of Mona's meds.
- Get new glasses for Mona and me.
- Get heart catheter done.
- Do a mother and daughter photo shoot. (I wanted Mona to have pictures to remind her of good memories in case something bad were to happen to me upon returning to the States like a heart attack or imprisonment.)
- Get my teeth checked one last time. (Again, I didn't know when I'd get back to the dentist.)
- Pick out my outfit for the arrest.
- Take Mona for karate classes.
- Say goodbye to all of my friends.
- Get one last pedicure done.
- Be on time for the plane's departure.
- Pray.

(My diary was full like this for the entire month before my departure. The next two days of my diary were only some notes about Mona and seeing that she was okay.)

Welcome Home Marsha

The skies are gray, and the kids have just picked me up from jail in downtown Phoenix. The raindrops are refreshing and spiritual. It's as though the water's baptizing me—assuring me that all is forgiven, all is new.

We head down Grand Avenue, going west to our new apartment in Peoria. I'm glued to the passing scenery outside the window.

"This is *my* country, *my hometown*," I mumble under my breath. "This is where I was raised. I can't believe I'm home."

"Well, Mom? How does it feel to be home?" my Shedi asks, grinning from ear to ear. His dream of having his mother and sister in America has finally come true.

"Amazing! I still can't believe it. I recognize so many places, but at the same time I feel like I'm a stranger to Phoenix."

I squeal like a little kid each time I see something that brings back a memory, like the lights at Grand Avenue, a Circle K, and a Dairy Queen.

We arrive at our new apartment. It looks sleek and beautiful from the outside. The grass and trees are well groomed. We park right in front of the main office, next to a delightful water fountain. I hear the trickles of water, refreshing and serene. We walk toward the apartment just opposite the fountain. I walk up the stairs, tired and still a bit jittery—jumpy even. I'm fearful that I may be arrested again. America has been a forbidden place for me for so long, and now I'm standing here with nothing to hide.

My son opens the door with a bouncy anticipation; he can't wait to show me everything that he's done. I enter the living room and the first thing I notice is wall-to-wall carpeting in the living room—with all of the boxes that I had sent over from UAE, stacked along its edges. An instant sense of belonging rings through me. I know inside those simple cardboard boxes are the fragments of my last twenty-two years. I may not own a home or acres of property, but I have experiences—lots of them—*unique* experiences, and cherished memories.

My son continues the tour with radiating excitement. He shows me all of the items that he's bought in preparation for my arrival: food, toiletries and even two full-sized beds—one for me and one for his sister. I'm so proud of him. He came through for me when I needed him most. (Yeah, he may have forgotten to call the attorney, but we all have a good laugh about that now.)

Exhausted from the last forty-eight hours, I excuse myself, go into my room, and shut the door. Silence. I'm really home. I walk over to the edge of the bed and plop down. I exhale with great relief and gaze out the window trying to take in my sudden reality that I am back. The scene will forever be engrained in my memory. Outside there are beautiful green trees, and an enormous American flag waving gracefully in the breeze—as though welcoming me home. Home to my heritage. Home to my family that I'd left so many years ago. I lie down on the bed and easily fall asleep. It's been a heck of a two days.

Phoenix

It's been nearly two years since my return. I'm happily working in the administrative department for an international company, thanks to a lovely lady who showed faith in me, (whose kindness I'll always be grateful for). I've also tried my best to mend the broken and burnt bridges that I previously left behind. I had my day in court, and spoke the truth for the first time about the abuse in my past. The sentencing judge felt that my daughter needed me more than the prosecutor needed me to be in jail, so he set my probation period.

I'm now rediscovering America and all of its opportunities every day. I've been focusing on my daughter, my writing, and giving back to the community that I left so many years ago. I'm throwing myself into causes that are dear to my heart—human rights, the awareness of domestic violence, and adult literacy. I've so thankful for all of those who have welcomed me back to this country with open arms. I've forgiven all that has happened in my past, but I will not forget.

Mona is going to college and getting the considerations in life that she needs. I'm so thankful to be here for her. I can't imagine how difficult the transition would have been for her without me. Each day she's discovering new ways in which to express her inner feelings—particularly in her art and writing. She's so amazing, and I'm so proud of her.

Shedi is working hard, studying and supporting his family. He tells me he loves coming home to his family each night. I'm so proud of the man that he's become.

But honestly, not everything turned out as I had hoped. We had some difficulties getting used to some things like the food, the water, and health insurance issues. And remember the business purchase that was in my to-do list? Well, I'm sad to say that we didn't do our homework well enough before purchasing it, and the seller was able to commit fraud with us. We couldn't make any money and had to close the business down within seven months of purchasing it. The man we bought it from got away with all of my money. It left me unable to pay any of the creditors back. I ended up with over $190,000 in debt, and had no choice but to file bankruptcy. I learned a steep and painful lesson.

One last thing before I wrap this chapter up. A true miracle happened when I was writing this book. Since I'd lost all of my family pictures over the years of travels, I contacted my family via the Internet for any pictures that I may be able to use in the book to give it a personal touch. A homeowner in Phoenix found three boxes of my mother's belongings and contacted me, asking if I'd like to have them, to which I responded with an enthusiastic "Yes!"

The boxes were filled with some amazing things: my mother's original birth certificate from 1942, a pair of her reading glasses, a picture of her as the editor of her high school newspaper, and my school pictures from first grade and up. Then—as if that was not amazing enough,—there were the two scrapbooks she'd compiled from her travels to Pakistan. They were chockfull of pictures of us together in Kalu, along with all of the newspaper clippings and letters that I'd sent to her from back in 1992. After opening the boxes, I stood in shock. *How did these things find me?*

Holding those items finally gave me the closure that I needed while, at the same time, it also drew me closer to my mother. I felt her presence in the room while holding each photo and looking into her eyes. I could hear her voice calling me *Sissie*. It was as if each item had been handpicked by her personally, and kept hidden safely until my return. *Thank you mom.*

Gallery

Mom, when she was the editor for her high school newspaper.
Columbus, Ohio. Around 1958.

Mom and I, in Phoenix, Arizona. 1970.

With mom and my brother and sisters. Bullsgap, Tennessee. 1980.

Me and my bestie, Pam, at church camp. Arizona. 1982.

Me and another bestie, Stanislava 2007, Al Ain, UAE

Mother and daughter photo shoot. Al Ain, UAE. 2013.

Mom's first trip to Kalu Kalan, Pakistan.

Mom's first trip to Kalu Kalan, Pakistan.

Me and my son, Shedi. Hazro, Pakistan.

The kids playing in our courtyard. Kalu Kalan. 1992.

Left: Notice the doorstop, a big rock. Right: Shedi and Mona ready to go to school. This is the main road from Hazro to Kalu Kalan. 1992.

Awesome pictures of the water pump where we did the dishes. Kalu
1992.

Amijon and Roni sweeping the mud during the rain. Kalu Kalan. 1992

The kids and I building a fireplace with a mixture of mud and cow dung.
Kalu Kalan. 1992.

Me and my favorite aunt, Peachy Massie. Kalu Kalan. 1992.

My bestie, Roni, and I during her wedding cerimonies. 2001.

My two adorable sons! Shedi's taken in 1992. Nudul's taken around 2010.

A sheet of my Urdu writing practice. 1992.

Laying the footings of my new home across from Amijon's house.

Amijon (left) cleaning out her cow dung room. Me with Bessie the cow (right).

My new home in Kalu (across from Amijon).
Front yard where I had the learning center.

My new home in Kalu (across from Amijon). Second story. Living
room(left). Shedi's room (right).

My new home in Kalu (across from Amijon). Living area on first floor, where the door's lock broke during the tornado.

My new home in Kalu (across from Amijon).
My kitchen on the first floor.

My new home in Kalu (across from Amijon).
View of the neighboring village from upstairs.

View of our village from atop of Amijon's house.

My son, Shedi, and his best friend, Abid, at Wadi Adventure getting ready
for some white water rafting.
Al Ain, UAE, 2012.

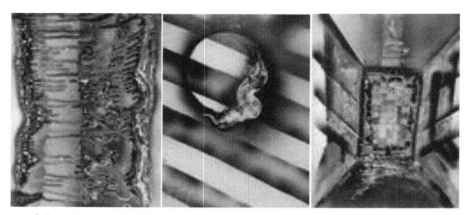

(Mona's artwork. She had two showings Pakistan, and a published painting in The Source Magazine, Al Ain, UAE in 2012.)

Marsha 'Yasmine' Marie has been a writer, human rights activist, English instructor and department head, American accent trainer, communication lab designer, voice-over talent, blogger, administrative assistant and mom. Born in Ohio, but raised in Arizona; Marsha lived and taught in Asia for over two decades. She has now returned to Arizona, and lives with her children. *BANGLES* is her self-publishing debut. Check out www.marshamarie.com for updates on upcoming titles in the *BANGLES* series.

Made in the USA
Columbia, SC
07 May 2017